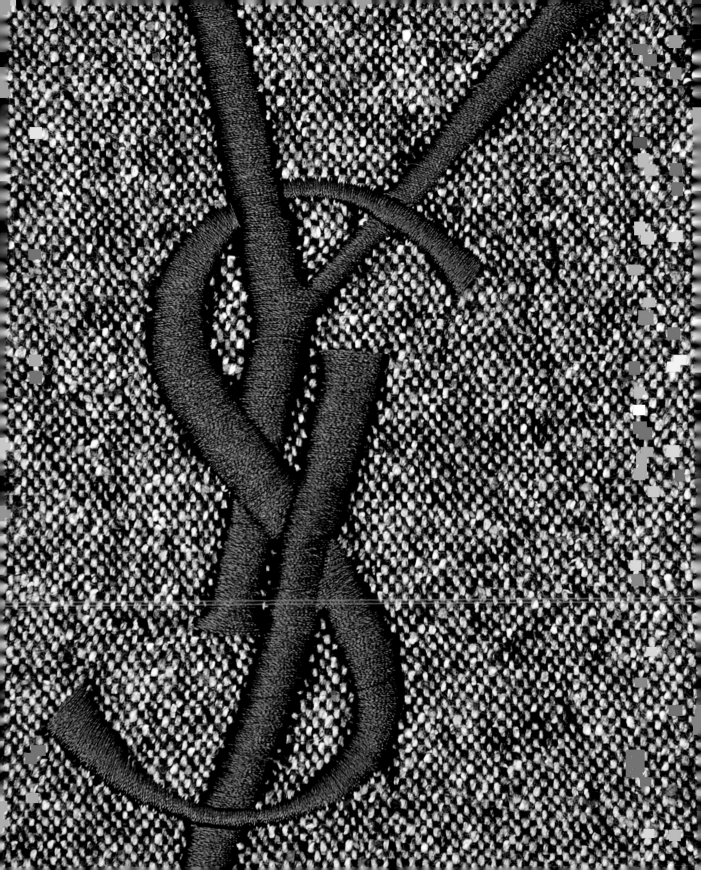

SERIES EDITED BY ÉLISABETH COUTURIER

CATHERINE SCHWAAB

talk about
fashion

Flammarion

PREFACE

I remember it well.

A taste for fashion begins with one's mother, with a certain idea of stylishness. Mine had her own dressmaker. Having a houndstooth suit made, she would dress her daughters in splendid A-line coats cut out of the same fabric, complete with red taffeta linings. I must have been six. But my very first sartorial emotion dates back even further: to her taxi cab-yellow tulle underskirt worn under a Brigitte Bardot dress. Gloriously princess-like, in a stiff, luminous material that crackled under the fingers. The only domain in which a little girl like me could give free rein to Cinderella-gown fantasies was my night-gown. It had froufrous, ribbons, patterns, and, most of all, it was *long*!

Illustrations for fairy tales, movie stills. At an age when high heels remained out of bounds, I would wait impatiently for the holidays in Italy and its markets to get my feet into a pair of *zoccoli*, tottering clogs (in sizes from the smallest up to eleven), in which I would clatter over the cobblestones. Bliss!

Op art was about to make its dazzling entrance into our neighborhood. But it turned out that shiny black-and-white coats were not available for children. The despair! Is this why I subsequently couldn't get enough of the jumble of 1970s fashion? Miniskirts, maxi-skirts, orange synthetics, Indian tunics, bell-bottoms, and corduroy. I remember, too, those first feverish purchases in Chelsea while on a language exchange in London: suede patchwork miniskirts and mini-sweaters that itched. I blush with shame to recall.

Fortunately, since then, many a retro vogue has sorted the classic wheat from the stylistic chaff. Countless trawls through secondhand clothing shops (words like "vintage" and "retro" were as yet unknown) soon taught me. Fabric, cut, lining, and style. A complete culture for so little cash. I combed the secondhand shops to avoid looking like everyone else.

Neither H&M nor Zara as yet ruled main street. Yet already "this season's must-have colors" got my goat. But with an eight dollar cashmere bubble coat (mildly moth-eaten, I must admit), I had my mitts on a collector's item for a song. I changed buttons, re-sewed hems and linings; I mixed and matched; I combined and crossed: like a real pro.

Since then, I've actually become a pro. I started out in the madcap 1980s covering Paris shows for the radio station Europe 1: Mugler and his daunting praying mantises, Montana and his leather-clad cinch-waists, Jean Paul Gaultier and his heady cross-gendering, Alaïa and his switchback dragonflies, Miyake all shimmer and sheen. And all this shock, dazzle, and head-scratching had to hit the airwaves at 7:30 in the morning for an audience that was not in the least interested in my impressions and enthusiasms. At the Cour Carrée shows (at the Louvre), I would bump into women's magazine staffers kitted out in black or minimal beige looking like Japanese designers, with straightened, flattened hair, no makeup and no smile. Is this how people reporting on fashion inevitably end up?

When I decided to jump ship and do a Masters in Fashion Management at the Institut Français de la Mode, it was with the firm intention of communicating my zeal and of earning a joyous living in the arcane world of high fashion. I discovered a passionate environment that was also, often, a battlefield. I learned the lot, grinding away in style bureaus where the sibyls of fashion turn out to be divas with feet of clay.

But nothing has eroded my love of fashion. The mounting excitement before a show, the pleasure in spotting a new style, the joy of stumbling across another vintage clothing store. The sleepless nights before an appointment: What to wear? I would mentally scan my closets unable to decide. There were mornings when my indeciveness meant I missed ten subway trains. But there could be no question of spending a day that would often stretch long into the night feeling badly dressed. But, deep down, what's all the effort *for*? Playing with dolls, my editor suggests. No, I for one don't play. It's much more serious than that.

ASTOUNDING
Intriguing
and attractive
combinations:
a Paul Smith
umbrella.

WHAT *IS* FASHION?

Fashion is like an anthology of stories about ourselves. You think it is superficial, consumerist, paradoxical, provocative, and fleeting? Maybe, but it also shows us the way we are, pigeonholing us without mercy. Are you a fashion victim? A fashion conquistador? Or maybe an anti-fashion militant? Perhaps you think you stand loftily above the flip-flop stylistic mêlée you read about in the magazines. Think again. Your brain perceives; it records. A misguided titillation of tulle and net? A skillful—or awkward—attempt to mix and match today's colors? The obvious difference between real dark Goth black and soft-pedaling Japanese-style black? You see it all.

Such distinctions (de)compose our perceptions. Fashion has invaded everything. You can run, but you can't hide. A pocket guide to anthropology, it speaks of its time, it trains the eye, it establishes templates to be adopted, and carves out codes of taste and distinction.

In the 1920s and 1930s, Jean Cocteau compared it to a kind of virus. His observations of the handbag fights between *Poiret-Belle-Époque* and *Chanel-la-Moderne* could be a novel: "Fashion dies so young. It lights us with a kind of phosphorescence, bringing a redness to the cheeks that moves us," he wrote. "It is condemned from birth. It almost died before living. It has only one chance to throw its bouquet, no more. It is both insolent and beguiling. One could define it thus: a merciless epidemic that makes people of diverse and opposite backgrounds obey a mysterious order from one knows not where that subjects them to practices that affect their own. . . . Until, that is, a new order is issued which changes the state of play and forces them to swap horses midstream."

This bizarre state of affairs fools no one. And yet, as trend follows trend, we give in to the most fleeting of passions. No sooner do you think you're in the swing than the wind turns. As if it had run out of steam, in less than a year that royal blue, those candy stripes you once adored are suddenly out. Wear them today and you'd look old hat. Worse: You wouldn't feel too good in them either. And so is another passing fancy consigned to the trashcan of history. **It has recently been claimed that the age of the fashion diktat is past. I'm not so sure. What was an iron-fist dictatorship has mollified into a soft tyranny. The way our tastes are guided today is more mysterious. Are we still being manipulated? Why do the most independently minded still yield to style crushes or betrayals? Is it because deep down we are so insecure that we have to adopt a specific "look"? To reassure ourselves?**

TONGUE-IN-CHEEK
The late Jean-Rémy Daumas was a much vaunted designer of the 1980s: joyous, crazy, ironic. He died of AIDS.

OH FASHION!

**Because fashion, with a hint of radi-
calism, keeps tribes apart. Nothing
more reassuring than recognizing oneself in a circle of initiates.**

In the eighteenth century, the philosopher Immanuel Kant observed that "to be strictly accurate fashion is not a matter of taste, but of pure vanity: of pretending to be a person of rank." The austere Protestant scoffed at the touching desire to be "in" as it generates a peacock's-tail race to imitation.

And what of our craving for lightness in a world whose grimness threatens to throttle all sense of play? It resurfaces in our pleasure in dressing up. Joining in these games of appearance brings out the child in all of us.

Never were women as inventive about their appearance as during World War II. With everything rationed—silk, linen, cotton, buttons, zippers, leather—body-hugging jackets of military severity were decorated with easy-to-find felt. As sequins were still available, they cropped up everywhere, to brighten a woolen garment, to illuminate an evening dress often cut of some raw, undyed fabric. Not to mention the accessories: platform soles in cork, wood, and tire treads, or clutch bags made of leather offcuts. Rather than give in to the shortages, French and English women "made do" and invented fashions as they went along. **So what *is* "fashion"? The French word *mode* comes from the Latin *modus* ("manner, measurement"), while the English "fashion" is a variant of French façon ("manner, way"). That is to say, an entire system including look, style, and trend; an outfit of (self-) exhibition that defines you *as* you.**

We cannot claim to be indifferent, to observe these "eternal rebirths" without obeying their injunctions. We are at once participant and witness. Who hasn't one day been charmed by the subtle harmony of an ensemble by Dries Van Noten, with its combination of perfect proportions and unexpected color scheme? Or been struck, even for an instant, by the impeccable fall of a Valentino dress, or by some particularly left-field accessory—gloves, shoes— or by a hat that knocks a classic . . . into a cocked hat? Curious or admiring, we all feel the power of fashionable attire: crisp elegance, radical style, retro charm, calculated lines, discreet sobriety, self-conscious extravagance. You can't ignore it. Fashion is a kind of movie in real-time.

The commentary Baudelaire offered in 1868 in *The Painter of Modern Life* on a sequence of fashion plates dating from the Revolution (1789) to the Consulate (1804) articulates a social appraisal.

"What I enjoy seeing in almost all these costumes is the morals and aesthetics of the period. Man's idea of the beautiful transpires in his every garment, crumpling or stiffening his attire, rounding off or straightening up his gestures, and even subtly penetrating, over time, his facial features. Man ends up resembling what he would like to be. These prints can be redrawn as beautiful or ugly; as ugly, they become caricatures; as beautiful, antique statues."

Proof positive that fashion unrolls in history like a thousand Proustian *madeleines*, complete with timeline. There are films one likes to watch over and over again, transfixed, just for the costumes and make-up: from *Ninotchka* to *Paris Frills*, from Vincente Minnelli to Ernst Lubitsch, not to mention on the *Star Wars* saga. To leaf through a family album is to undergo a fashion flashback: our mother's coat dress, our primary school smock, Jackie Kennedy's suits, a (Grace) Kelly bag by Hermès, our first Thierry Mugler jacket. **A vanished world comes back onto focus little by little, unremitting—not quite our own, but not entirely unlike it either.**

ACCORDION
MADNESS
Designers Viktor &
Rolf, for whom each
show is an event,
exaggerate and
redefine, always
tottering on the
edge and forcing
us to relearn how
to look.

REVOLUTION
ON THE RUNWAY
Diane Von Furstenberg
in the 1970s. Cool,
calm, and collected
models present her
famous wrap dress.

FACING PAGE
PROVOCATIVE!
Every season,
for many designers
(here Jean Paul
Gaultier in the
2000s) certain
pieces just serve
to set the tone for
a show—humor,
eroticism, the
1940s—so they are
sure to feature on
the fashion pages.

FASHION: A NEW CONCEPT?

You might be forgiven for thinking that fashion is a phenomenon of the modern era that has attained its maximum exposure in our consumer society. On the contrary: Fashion extends back into prehistory. Primitive man sported signs, paintings on the skin, and he gauged his power by his adornment. Self-decoration meets an elemental need, more fundamental even than the necessity of protecting the body.

Tribal "fashion."
A headman of
the Logo tribe (Congo)
in 1926. Musée
du Quai Branly, Paris.

Yes, fashion reaches back into prehistory, to before 5000 BCE. Man made his entrance ready tattooed and ready pierced, at once sacred, mystic, and decorative. In the Italian Alps, and from Egypt to Japan, the discovery of mummified bodies confirms it: traces of skin-deep inscriptions are found everywhere. In Europe, the Gauls, the Germans, and the Picts of Britain all succumbed to this drive to mark their artistic sensibility on themselves, while in New Zealand the Maori adorned their body to receive grace and protection from their "guardian angel." In Japan, as in Polynesia, tattoos and scarifications confirm rank and power.

FACING PAGE
The expressive
body: samurai,
yet contemporary.
Musée Guimet,
Paris.

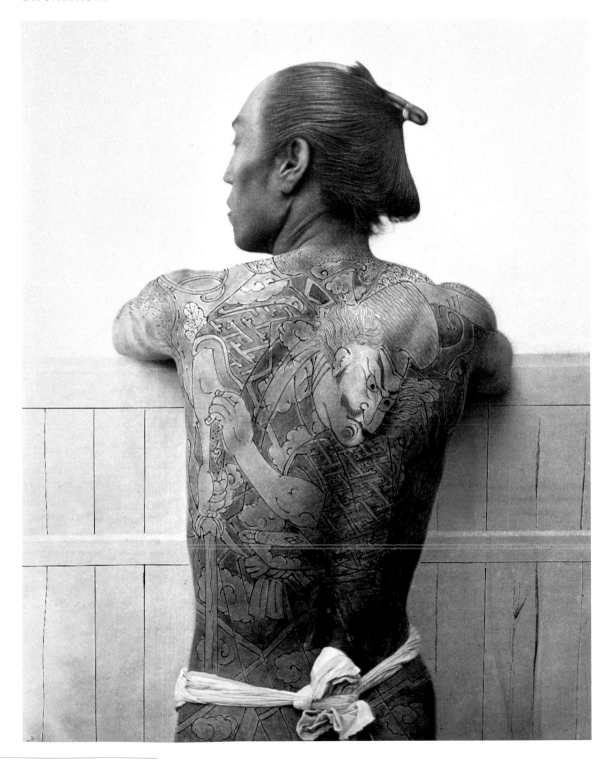

Stranger still: in Thailand and Burma, the famous brass spiral necklace of the "giraffe women" remains a tradition whose roots are lost in the mists of time. (It does not break the neck vertebrae, as has been claimed, but lowers the shoulders and ribs.)

In Africa and Amazonia, self-decoration is completed by lip plates. Over the centuries, man has never lost this taste for ornamentation. At the beginning of the Christian era, Rome outlawed the practice of tattooing as it deemed it pagan, but this did not prevent pilgrims to Jerusalem from having a cross indelibly carved into their skin as a kind of testimonial.

In every culture, and through the ages, these signals, far from being incidental, were identifiers. The outward signs of an ordeal whose sufferings had been endured, as during an initiation. It was this ambiguity—contradictory feelings of curiosity and fear—that attracted crowds in London in 1769. The famously tattooed Captain James Cook had returned from his Tahitian expedition with a certain "Prince Omai": the many tattoos he had earned for valor launched a brief fashion among the courtesans of the British capital.

The English seem, moreover, to have been connoisseurs in this domain, as the tradition goes back much further than that. One of the first nobles to wear tattoos was born in 1022: King Harold II. It is no coincidence that the finest tattoo artists work in London. Later sovereigns too—Edward VII, George V, and George VI—were not above having a dragon or other emblem emblazoned on their skin. Then there was Churchill, rolling up his sleeves at the Yalta Conference to reveal an anchor, a souvenir of his feats in the navy. Stalin and Franklin D. Roosevelt belonged to the same brotherhood, too: the former had a death's-head on his chest, the latter, the family crest.

As art historian Thomas Golsenne explains concerning animist societies, self-decoration and ornament function as a kind of social passport: "The importance of a man can be measured by his decorative power, i.e., by his ability to affect, to impinge on a wide circle of relationships.... This is indispensable to anyone desirous of earning a position in the society. It is a sign of recognition." One might say the same thing today about a solid gold watch, of a python-skin boot, or of a piercing or tattoo.

For many years the preserve of "hard" men—of sailors, yakuzas, truck-drivers—these epidermal adornments exude an air of toughness, or else of transsexuality or sadomasochism. The mark of the outsider or the dissident, they generated rejection or fear. One had to await the advent of a conspicuous gay community before they acquired their status as pure ornament. Symbolic, refined, and artistic. Body piercing, once carefully confined to parts of the physique concealed from public view, has "come out"—on nostrils, eyebrows, tongues, cheeks, navels, and nipples. As a tribal marker, a piercing catalogs you as easily as yesterday's pearl necklace or signet ring: rocker (dark nails, big rings), eco warrior (little snake, leaf), or romantic (heart and arrow, treble clef). Whatever it is can be taken out and the hole closes up. A tattoo is something else again: It lasts.

The desire "to brand oneself with the iron" is curious. Beyond the elemental need for ornament and sign, could it be the harbinger of a new animism? A test of one's resistance to pain? A cry of defiance against the transitoriness of all things? Fashion against the old-fashioned? Tattooing restores the gravity of origins.

READY TO PARTY
Baroque, bejeweled,
and tattooed,
a mildly S&M
poet sports
a skirt and
necklaces for
Jean Paul Gaultier,
a designer
who always
enjoys playing
with sexual
conventions.

EIGHTEENTH-
CENTURY GLORIES
A gown á la
française, in silk
and satin, as worn
at the French court
in about 1740–50.
The motifs are
woven into the
material and overkill
does not seem to
have been a major
worry. Musée
Historique des
Tissus, Lyon.

NUIT DE CHINE
Much taken with
art deco, French
designer Paul Poiret
not only liberated
woman from the
shackles
of the corset in
1906, but also
brought a touch
of the exotic to
collections inspired
by orientalism,
Russia, and Africa.

FACING PAGE
REPORTING
FOR DUTY
Thierry Mugler was
the emblematic
designer of the
"wonder women,"
the "go-getters"
of the 1980s,
here strapped into
military uniforms
with oversize
shoulders and
narrow waists.

OH FASHION!

FASHION: WHAT'S IT FOR?

Fashion fulfills many functions, from the most obvious to the least apparent. It serves (partly) as covering, (often) as self-embellishment, and (most definitely) as a social identifier. Since its early development, it has served all these purposes, but especially the last: to proclaim one's rank. In the Middle Ages, for example, the richer and more powerful you were, the more ostentatious and expensive was your apparel. In European courts, then in the fledgling democracies, it also indicated one's position on the social ladder.

Even after World War II, appearances were still conditioned by tacit vestimentary rules: there were "blue collars" (manual workers) and "white collars" (office staff). The distinction was clear even outside the world of work. A lack of financial means or sartorial experience was perceptible at a glance. On vacation, a time of freedom and nonchalance, the bourgeoisie could be distinguished perfectly from the proletariat, artists from tradesmen, and business leaders from the middle classes. Each dressed according to his status, age, and circumstance. Moreover, this is how couture houses came up with sport, casual, and cruise collections. **We have the impression that today all these conventions have been shattered. Fashion has been democratized, it straddles the generations, and those in the know are not the same as before.**

From Galliano's red-hot collection for Dior to the most recent arrivals in Zara, not forgetting collectors' designer pieces for H&M, Mango, Top Shop, or New Look, or the new Indian and Chinese designers, those who know about fashion are no longer just the highfliers. The most feared criticism no longer comes from the great and the good. The new arbiters of elegance are as often to be found in the school playground or in squats as on the fashion pages. The boot of power is now on the other foot: fashion culture has become a deadly weapon. And the favorite sport on café terraces or in editorial meetings is to point the finger at the most egregious faux-pas of our celebrities and leaders. It has to be said that the codes have become much more complicated since that benign, long-gone era when *Elle*,

"AT MY AGE"
In 2009, the brand The Kooples broke with the cult of youth by employing (real) senior couples to model their rock outfits. More power to their elbow.

Marie Claire, and *Vogue* were able to pronounce that the fashion was "length," "padded shoulders," or "false blacks." **Thirty, forty, fifty years ago, and more, everything was so simple: there was *one* fashion and that was that. If one wanted to be in, one didn't have much choice: it was *that* cut, *that* length, *those* materials.**

Or one climbed up to the giddy heights of one's idols by slavishly imitating their get-up. Elvis's quiff, Marilyn's blonde curls, Jane Fonda's dramatic eyeliner, Romy Schneider's chignon, Jackie Kennedy's darkglasses, as well as Bogart's raincoat, Rock Hudson's tuxedo, Marcello Mastroianni's pleated pants, Lauren Bacall's Bar suit, Liz Taylor's cardigan, Monica Vitti's flouncy dress, Brigitte Bardot's ballet flats, Catherine Deneuve's black PVC coat, Marlon Brando's skintight T-shirt, or James Dean's jeans.

One would call one's dressmaker and get a copy run up or make for a department store, and in a flash one was in style. And one was conscious of reaching the hallowed portals of the patron saints of elegance. Today, the reflex to ape is no less present, but it has become more critical: one eschews faithful imitation for fear of passing for a groupie. One selects, adapts, arranges, customizes. Michael Jackson's red military jacket? It's worn oversize and torn or in white. Audrey Hepburn's iconic little black dress? Slip on a pair of fuchsia pantyhose underneath, or wear it over shorts, or under a leather biker jacket. Can't afford Ines de la Fressange's Chanel jacket? Get your hands on a copy at a market and sew on a length of sequined braid. **Because fashion is also an essential expression of our freedom. One is no longer "branded" by one's origins or social class. No, fashion, "your" fashion confers a feeling of belonging. Do you wear a skinny tie out clubbing? Do you sport a (real or fake) Kelly (the legendary Hermès bag) with your jeans or pencil skirt? You spoil yourself with Adidas designed by Yohji Yamamoto? Do you have a vintage Courrèges dress? You like the all-black look? You thus appear in the world as you, and you alone, decree. It's like being born again! Fashion: What power!**

ADIDAS SNEAKERS
Every six months or so, sports brands bring out new models for clubbing or popping wheelies that soon vanish from the shelves. (They are copied just as quickly.)

ETERNAL,
TRANSPARENT
Belgian minimalist
Ann Demeulemeester
is devoted to black
in all its shades and
textures. Here,
chiffon and jersey
overlay.

FACING PAGE
FLASHY
On the other hand,
the Spaniard Agatha
Ruiz de la Prada is
not afraid of using
colors and patterns
in a girly style whose
"philosophy" she is
happy to embrace.

FASHION: WHO MAKES IT?

Who lurks behind that tapering silhouette, that geometric block, that androgynous smile? Internationally known designers, that's who. But although planet fashion today glimmers with labels and names as famous as movie stars, this has not always been the case.

There was a time when the empress, nobles, and wielders of power decided what they'd wear themselves. Master dressmakers carried out their wishes and would never have allowed themselves to arrive with an off-the-peg model. That is until an Englishman by the name of Charles Frederick Worth tired of the game. He was the first to have the idea of opening a couture house in Paris, at 7 rue de la Paix.

The objective: trends would no longer be dictated by his customers as if to some common tailor. He would impose his on them. "My work is not to execute. It is above all to invent. I don't want people ordering their clothing. I will propose it to them." The year was 1858 and Worth was thirty-one years old.

He'd trained in London, but very quickly realized that real style happened in Gay Paris, the epicenter of *la mode*. Aged twenty he left the English capital to join Gagelin's, a Parisian draper whose fabrics, trinkets, shawls, and capes sold like hot cakes. For the sales assistant Marie Vernet—who was to become his wife—he made austere and less ornamented dresses that met with enthusiasm from his customers. The age was still trapped in the overblown corseted silhouette of the Victorian age. But the Belle Époque was on the horizon: twists, froufrous, and an "S"-line strangled in a corset. Women would pass out during dinner. Worth kept the corset, but he softened the line, while the flounces, jabots, topstitching, and lace all became less invasive. He had the cheek to insist that the aristocracy and high society come to his salons where his designs would be presented on models. In this way he won over Princess Metternich with a silver-embroidered white tulle evening gown. Dazzled, Empress Eugénie chose him as her exclusive supplier. International fame followed: Worth dressed the czarina of Russia, the queen of Italy, Empress Elizabeth of Austria, and Queen Victoria. For the first time, fashion was ordained by one man. Acknowledged as an artist, a designer was no longer a lowly craftsman: he was now a creative artist and could sign his wares. Whose prices, inevitably, gained a few zeros.

FACING PAGE
MAESTRO GALLIANO!
At each show,
the head of the house
of Dior John Galliano
throws himself
into the spirit
of the collection:
the eighteenth
century, horsewomen,
courtesans. Here, at
the emperor's grand ball,
a dashing *chevalier*.

While Worth launched the business, it was the Frenchman Paul Poiret who was its most creative scion. His idea: to break the yoke, to sweep away sixty years of distortion by crinoline, corset, and whalebone. Instinctively, Poiret invented a silhouette in step with the social changes underway: natural and mobile, it liberated women.

The couturier learned drawing from Jacques Doucet, bookworm and rival of Worth's, a friend of the painters Degas and Monet, and a collector of Van Gogh, Léger, and Miró. Poiret never lost this keen taste for modern art and it shows in his geometrical and unfussy lines. He turned to artists such as Raoul Dufy and Paul Iribe, thus paving the way for the frequent collaboration between couture and the decorative arts. He thus did away with the corset and invented a high waist inspired by Directoire style. Small bust, drapes, and slits down the sides to make walking easier. This was in 1906, with his wife as his model, in between five pregnancies. The way was open. The Paquin house, the Callot sisters, and, above all, foreigners opened salons in the French capital, giving free rein to their creativity, erecting the first pillars of "haute couture": Brits like Redfern, Creed, Lucile, and Molyneux, the American Mainbocher, the Spaniards Balenciaga and Castillo, the Swiss Robert Piguet, the Italian Elsa Schiaparelli, and the Greek Jean Dessès.

Thus began a reign that was to last for more than a hundred years: houses whose reputation rose and fell with the name of designers who cultivated a legendary world of dreams. Today things have changed. Haute couture is a shop-window with an artistic laboratory attached. Surrounded by virtuoso craftsmen, the couturier can let his imagination run riot without concerning himself with profit.

Thanks to the head seamstresses, pattern makers, cutters, toilemakers, embroiderers, and plumassiers, thanks to these nimble fingers all working in the shadows, masterpieces now appear that may be presented just once in public, and then vanish into a warehouse.

But these dream dresses costing 30,000, 50,000, even 500,000 dollars will be seen in photographs all over the world: better than any publicity campaign. Complex and opulent, a haute couture collection is picked over to inspire every element of the brand. Exoticism, 1950s, or futurism—a few straps there, an asymmetric twist here, an unlikely association of colors, a shower of nails, a ballet of fringes or flounces. A show by Gaultier or Galliano is pored over like the seismograph of some sociological earth tremor. Where did they get their inspiration this time? Vintage? Sport? Off the street? At the movies? From technology, pop, or folklore? In homeopathic doses, these stylistic leads percolate down to ready-to-wear and into cruise collections, into sportswear and knitwear lines, not to mention accessories. Because a fashion house, today, feeds into the powerful economic sector of luxury goods. In France, for example, income from luxury goods is second only to that generated by the aeronautics industry.

Unlike their predecessors who trained as simple tailors, contemporary couturiers need more than one string to their bow: they go to art school or graduate from some prestigious French, English, or American fashion school, they have to put up with internships as assistants—or even as the designer-cum-slave of the master—and absorb the principles of marketing as well as the arts of management.

Armani—one of the few to actually sell his haute couture—orchestrates his collections with the skill of one who knows his clients through and through. Thanks to a portfolio of trend-forecasting bureaus, the maestro keeps almost a dozen lines afloat. Recognizing the importance of the youth market at an early stage, he launched Armani Jeans before any other house thought of doing the same. On the other hand, the talented Christian Lacroix made the mistake of thinking he could keep going with nothing more than haute couture and luxury prêt-à-porter impregnated with baroque flamboyance. By letting his second lines slip, he neglected a potential economic powerhouse.

Observers reckon that after ten years in the trade, a designer starts copying himself. But that's often what his loyal customers require of him. Alaïa—the only one to make no true distinction between haute couture and prêt-à-porter—would soon lose customers if he unwisely dropped his sexy knit dresses, his perfect frock coats, or his narrow-fitting tight-busted jackets.

By relaunching his loose jackets every season with hardly an alteration, Armani is simply keeping the market happy. And what about Diane Von Furstenberg's eternal wrap dress? Moreover, today—thanks to the vintage trend—many designers reissue historic pieces from ten, twenty, or thirty years ago.

The self-confident Gabrielle Chanel once decreed: "I do not make fashion. I am fashion." Yet she still agonized about not being in the swing. But prior to becoming the high priestess of style, this modest *modiste* started out as a "militant": when a young designer, she simply couldn't afford all the paraphernalia of froufrous worn in the evening, at the races, or the theater. Liberating the line with fluid and less fussy dresses and jersey, she put women in pants, stripping the suit of its embroidery and elaborate collars and creating a no-frills template. A great leap forward into modernity. Just as "committed," when Jean Paul Gaultier unveils corsets, skirts for men, and religious imagery down a catwalk, he is not issuing a fashion diktat: he is taking up a position as an artist. Of modest origin, and gaining much of his inspiration from the street, Gaultier subscribes to a sociological tendency.

Thus, the "gurus" of fashion have changed sides: It's no longer aristocrats who set the trends. Journalists, bloggers, impertinent commentators, and photographers with an eye for a look enter the fray, tracking down new prophets to consecrate— or condemn.

This intuitive race can reduce one to panic. At the beginning of each season the transfer market bubbles in fashion, just like in soccer: will such and such a designer remain in house X despite a decline in sales? Or will the talented goose that lays the golden eggs of *maison* Y be poached by a rival team? Such business maneuvers seriously disturb brand identity. Remove its master and it may float uncertainly—as was all too obvious when Tom Ford left Gucci, Hedi Slimane left Dior Homme, and, especially, when Yves Saint Laurent quit his own firm.

To last, the hallmark of a true creator is to be irreplaceable.

BOLD AS BRASS
Madonna's sexual
provocation was
aided and abetted
by the style
trademarks of Jean
Paul Gaultier, who
made the costumes
for her tours and
public appearances.

FACING PAGE
Gabrielle Chanel
in the 1920s–30s,
a period still in the
thrall of frippery and
flounces, dared to
indulge in sporty
"masculine" jersey
and mixes of prints,
as well as pants
and fake pearls.

WHO'S THE CLIENT?
LOOKS CHANGE

No need to be a model or a global icon to win status as a trailblazer. Today, everyone is free to create his or her own look. Or non-look. If our outfits no longer proclaim our origins or social class, they still betray our personality. To pour one's curves into an eye-catching, eye-popping spray-on like the voluptuous Beth Ditto is still a style. The ostentatious dismissal of style says as much about our "profile" as a pronounced taste for the work of a given designer.

Besides movie and showbiz stars, the street can also launch a trend. In fact the street is a veritable gold mine. This has been understood very well by those many labels whose publicity campaigns turn to "real people."
Benetton launched a worldwide casting stunt to uncover "the new looks and faces of the twenty-first century." The appeal sounds like an SOS: "We're looking for somebody different, original, surprising." Beyond the marketing opportunity, the operation acknowledges the street as a place where style happens.

Less obviously, other labels have arranged castings for the general public to add punch to their ads. Petit Bateau and their legendary T-shirts were given a new lease of fashion life and an original touch with false photo-booth snaps of "real people" of all ages. The same year, a new label, The Kooples, kept ahead of the field by hiring pairs of friends, posing them awkwardly in front of the camera as if to say: "Hey, we're young, we're like you." Phony populism, if you like, that serves to cultivate a form of elitism between initiates.

This is all a far cry from the "socialite" years of the 1960s, 1970s, 1980s, and 1990s, when well-heeled women, idle heiresses, and rich men's wives set the tone in elegance and ensured a collection would be seen in all the best houses.
First off: Nan Kempner, the irresistible and witty New Yorker, heiress to a wealthy Ford dealer and wife of the owner of an investment bank, confessed she was "a clotheshorse" and

NO PROBLEM
The irresistible Beth Ditto turns her voluptuous form into a style statement as influential as the Kate Moss look.

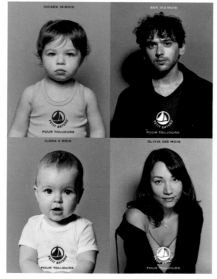

JUST LIKE YOU AND ME
Petit Bateau adverts display "photo-booth" snaps of "real people." Has the street taken over?

a shopaholic. "I spend way more than I should and way less than I want."
An exquisite hostess who loved soirées and kept going until the small hours,
informed us that the best moment of a party "is before it starts, when one
slips on the dress." She died in 2005, aged seventy-five, and did much for
the career of Yves Saint Laurent; as did the Lebanese Mouna Ayoub, a
true patron saint of high fashion. Wallis Simpson meanwhile, coined the
incomparable "never too rich or too thin," and more recently, Daphne
Guinness, a fan of Alaïa, sallies forth with her well-born friends from yacht
to five-star hotel. This brewery heiress is truly one of the last to take on this
subtle role of customer fashion icon who does not need to work to live,
and buys her wardrobe at full price. Ordinary mortals borrow them (haute
couture for a debutantes' ball), while actresses or singers seal a contract
with the house.

The search for a muse has become an intense but high-risk strategy for fashion houses seeking increased visibility: Vanessa Paradis, Nicole Kidman, Anna Mouglalis, and Lily Allen for Chanel, for example; Scarlett Johansson for Dolce & Gabbana or Madonna for Vuitton—the jury is out on whether this select band has won over many potential customers.

On the red carpet or in a cocktail party overrun by photographers, one has to show one can live in a garment. To feel it, to give it life, to match it to one's personality. Sirens do not grow on trees. Rather than just a good figure, what you need to impose a look is a "fashion icon personality."

But do such luxury clotheshorses, these follow-my-leader fashionistas, still set the tone? Don't trends, today, come instead from below, from the street? As revenge on all the diktats, all the good taste, the perfect styling. In these days of the web and of sampling, we each work on our appearance as if in a new global ballgame. You can pick something here, something else there, the choice is vast.

Are you a bit showbiz? A tree-hugger? Classy? Metrosexual? Vintage? Lolita? Preppy? Gangsta? *Sapeur?* The question is purely one of style. Adopting a look is a game. It's pushing a style to the brink of disguise. This though is not the same as "having style" (see page 44). It's less stable. More humorous and provocative. Rarely low profile. Your look can be based on an almost political slogan ("No Style," "Too Much," "No Logo"), on a pastime (skateboarding, tecktonik, rock music, art, Goth), on a way of life (hippie, Ivy League, hedonist), or just on the desire to be noticed.

Guidebooks have been written as an aid to identifying the sociotypes among this tirelessly proliferating and constantly renewed jungle of styles. One of the best and the funniest, the French *Dictionnaire du look* by Géraldine de Margerie and Olivier Marty, lists brands and ideas, preferences and habitats, obligations and prohibitions belonging to each type.

To create a look is a complex mission and there's many a pitfall, with the fashion police around the corner never slow to snigger. Not least photographers, who spend the best part of their lives on the lookout for wardrobe malfunctions. You want to be mentioned in dispatches? Hang out in a place where your vision will be appreciated for what it is. Create and don't back down! And, finally, a look really is a question of authority. And imagination.

"SEXY-ROCK"
A style immortalized by Géraldine de Margerie's *Dictionnaire du look*, a clever blend of second hand finds to create an ironic femininity: a polka-dot slip of a dress with a scarf round the waist clashes with the leather biker jacket, beanie, and fingerless gloves.

ON STYLE:
YOU EITHER HAVE IT . . .

This is an existential question on Planet Fashion: Do you have style or not? Because it is style that gives one distinction, far more than the wallet. It's all about carrying it off, that's obvious enough. And in this respect, Paris definitively has a thing or two to teach us. There's no gainsaying it: the Parisian (man or woman) knows how to dress. But whether this is because of their education, life story, geographical or social environment, curiosity or preferences; or just that subliminal experience founded on centuries of vamping, of razor-sharp eyes, and corrosive put-downs. Nothing can be more pitiless than the autopsy of an evening out in the French capital. And fashion occupies a predominant place. An error in taste is like meat-market swearing at an uptight meeting or passé slang at a rock gig. It gets remembered.

When, in *Les Petites Filles modèles*, the Comtesse de Ségur ridicules Madame Fichini for turning up at a picnic bedecked with ribbons and lace, she is taking a pot-shot at the dual "social indignity" of wearing garments both unsuited to the circumstances and ostentatious with respect to the sober canons of the good people of the time. Today, the same worry about feeling under- or overdressed—that is, about appearing out of step with contemporary custom—persists. The risks are limited if one relies on understatement, enriched by an accessory noticeable enough to shake up its minimalism. Because a "calculated defect is no bad thing. To exist in perfection results in boredom." In his treatise on elegance, Balzac had no hesitation in referring to innate grace: "A man becomes rich; he is born elegant."

For foreign designers, showing in Paris is to take the risk of falling flat on their face in what is a sophisticated and unforgiving microcosm. In interviews a few years ago,

Donna Karan tells how she instinctively noted a shift between American "casual" fashion (i.e., simple, easy-to-wear and not too elaborate) and French *mode*, more whimsical, more personal, more "special." To be admitted among the happy few of *créateurs* needs more originality than the Seven Easy Pieces she invented in the 1980s—seven garments combined throughout the day and even evening (pants, skirt, jacket, blouse, coat, etc.). A practical but tedious idea, at the very antipodes of the Parisian approach that is to swap accessories over a black number at the workplace, at lunch, and out in the evening.

What makes a style? A sartorial signature. Not just, nor necessarily, prettiness and class. Rather a kind of unshakable confidence in one's appearance.

FACING PAGE
MORE THAN MEETS THE EYE
Designed by Isabelle Marant, a look that goes one better than understatement: deadpan but with unquestionable sex appeal, a flawlessly natural complexion, but with the humorous accessory of an English bowler hat in an unusual shade. And a non-hairstyle which *is* a hairstyle, to counteract any residual archness.

OH FASHION!

The sociologist Bruno Remaury, director of design at the Institut Français de la Mode, references dandyism: "Since the Renaissance, distinction by appearance is a challenge; thus, clothing reveals the talent of its wearer." It was George Bryan Brummell, the famous "Beau Brummell" who, at the beginning of the nineteenth century, was crowned Prince of Dandies. The son of a private secretary, he showed with panache that nobility was more a question of taste than of pedigree. This is even truer today.

Dandy chic? Not to attract attention, while exuding a certain something that imposes a style.

Brummell wrote down his ideas in a *Book of Fashion*: a full-fledged theory of sartorial elegance that also addresses female dress, emphasizes harmonious colors (he preferred discreet tones, black, brown, navy), and on the relations between attire and architecture.

To have style can be a matter of adopting certain hallmarks, as when you interlard constructions inspired by the narrow-fitting jackets of Dior-Galliano, Yohji Yamamoto asymmetries, or the graphic lines of Cardin-Courrèges. Or of going in for strange associations of colors, like Dries Van Noten, a virtuoso of strange hybrids. His colors are never really "fashionable." Seldom bright and yet luminous, they are rooted in a kind of timeless cachet. One can choose the androgyny of Charlotte Gainsbourg, the sober-natural black-white-ecru of Charlotte Rampling, or the black monochrome set off by jewels of Franca Sozzani, editor in chief of *Vogue Italia*.

On the other hand, Anna Wintour, editor in chief of American *Vogue*, owes her style more to her blonde bob and her pout than to her last-collection-by-XYZ little black dresses that smack of clothes-hanger marketing.

Style is a vestimentary personality imprinted on every circumstance that identifies you more easily than your favorite label.

A girl perpetually in Alaïa or Chanel does not inevitably *have* style. She has just invested in blue-chip stock. She has learned the code book of these designers without question, without criticism. It's a practical uniform. Such lazy choices by a woman insecure of her style are described by novelist Marguerite Duras: "I've had a uniform for now on fifteen years. It's the M. D. uniform. Last year, this uniform, which has generated, it appears, a 'Duras look,' was taken up by a couturier: black waistcoat, straight skirt, turtleneck

sweater and short winter boots. The search for a uniform equates to that for a unity between form and content, between what one thinks one looks like and what one would like to look like, between what one thinks one is and what one wants to hint at by wearing what one wears. One finds it without really looking for it. And once found, it's final. And it ends up by defining you. At last: that's done! One's comfortable." Unlike for Duras, for you cultivating a style has been an endless, uphill task. Over the years, you've had to adapt the trends in your own way, with that added personal touch that evinces critical judgment, not blind obedience, or negligence.

To *have* style means to go against the grain. It means saying "No" or "Yes, but ..."

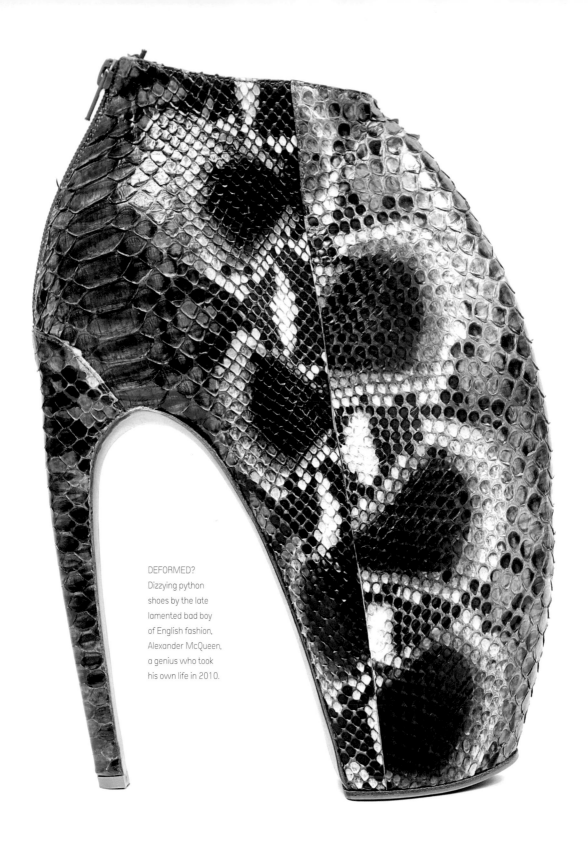

DEFORMED?
Dizzying python
shoes by the late
lamented bad boy
of English fashion,
Alexander McQueen,
a genius who took
his own life in 2010.

IF YOU LIKE . . .

IF YOU LIKE . . .

ECCENTRIC

Your psychosocial profile

In geometry, "eccentric" means "that which deviates from the center." In more human terms: you, the eccentric, constantly try to make yourself conspicuous, to "stand out." You crave attention. For you, a truly disastrous evening is one when no one makes a remark—whether admiring or catty, bittersweet or mocking—about you.

Because the eccentric sweats blood over her appearance. So nothing could be more frustrating than to pass unnoticed, to fail to break the barriers of decency and propriety of those who can see you, but say nothing. Even worse is when you can't detect the least glimmer of surprise in their eyes.

Luckily, when they show up at your place, you are invariably gratified by their amazement as they gaze open-mouthed at your apartment's Venetian carnival decor.

To devise a look—or the idea behind it—the eccentric has to get to know the opposite camp by heart. What are you *not* in the center of? Well, conventions, classicism, sobriety, preppiness, the smart set—and their finer feelings. So you have to know the complete repertory of your adversaries' codes. The more you frequent ordinary circles, the easier you'll find it to cultivate eccentricity.

FACING PAGE
BRITISH EXTRAVAGANZA
Taken separately, each piece in this Alexis Mabille outfit is almost traditional. It's the bold juxtapositions that make it so unusual.

LEFT
ALICE IN WONDERLAND
In the screen version directed by Tim Burton (2010) with costumes by Colleen Atwood, Johnny Depp plays a magical Mad Hatter.

Your icons

Perhaps the French eighteenth-century *merveilleuses* and *incroyables*—radical dressers who, reacting against the canons of post-Revolutionary beauty, dabbled in a carefully concocted blend of down-at-heel and baroque medievalism. More recently, the films of Monty Python, John Woo, and Tim Burton provide rich pickings for your unbridled imagination.

Your style

The polar opposite of purity and sobriety. You like strange colors, prints, and materials, retro— a goldmine for everything left-field—bizarre concoctions, and accessories from goodness knows where.

Your notion of what is becoming is not without piquancy: as you are far from averse to provocation, you are capable of turning up at a dinner dressed in an astute assemblage of refuse bags adorned with costume jewelry, or in a retro fishnet bathing suit, a tuxedo jacket, and thighboots, or else a sublime Galliano jacket with embroidered basque over a pair of skirts in eye-popping colors. Back home, imagination takes precedence over standard issue "elegance": unabashed by your curves, you display them in plunging necklines and skintight dresses. The most important thing in the end is to attract attention to your discoveries.

The designer who has promoted eccentricity as a style is Vivienne Westwood, ex-1970s punk. Her motto: "You have a much better life if you wear impressive clothes." She is the absolute embodiment of her style: red hair and milk-white skin, long-line bustier dress and tartan-print crinolines assembled into complex, clashing constructions.

With scant regard to functionality—like you—she adores giant platform soles. If you can't afford her creations, so much the better. Let your imagination run riot and set a trend scoured from the flea markets or by designers newly graduated from fashion schools.

Play fast and loose with some oilcloth found in a hypermarket store, get hold of the buoyant colors of Agatha Ruiz de la Prada, the surrealist, dream-like hats of Marie Mercié, some Gap Kids' scarves and hats, and customize. The eccentric knows how to ply a needle and thread: sew, frill, shorten, add a fluorescent tassel here, change the buttons there.

ECCENTRIC

Her essentials

Focus on unusual materials and prints: a tapestry coat or ivory, red, or turquoise fur. Work on your accessories: an immense scarf in dazzling taffeta; bucketfuls of quart-size jewels; colored, patterned pantyhose; and layers of socks. As to makeup: false lashes and teasing and back-combing, heavy highlights. It's up to you how extravagant you go, according to the effect required. One can be eccentric without looking like a Christmas tree. Customization counts too: you can thread a length of Hermès (or Chanel, or Dior) packing ribbon round your jeans as a belt, for example. Just for fun.

INSPIRED BY SWING
Musical graphics,
clashing colors,
but a toned-down
palette. Vintage
sweater and tie,
with agnès b. pants.

STRIPES!
WITH PLAID!
The harlequinade
of the vintage dress
brings out the lines
on the Moschino
jacket and Promod
scarf. And a
Borsalino always
makes a statement.

BACK FROM INDIA
It all depends how
the colors are put
together: the pale
pink coat adorned
with gold thread
by Antik Batik, the
almost fluorescent
taffeta belt, and
turquoise raw-silk
pants, the whole
topped off by a
gigantic Dries Van
Noten necklace.

This kind of look can't be bought off the shelf;
one has to compose it for oneself.
Such ideas are simply hints, avenues for further experiments.

IF YOU LIKE . . .

AFRICAN QUEEN
The madcap leopard
print is pursued in
similarly fun tones:
beige, camel, gold,
bronze, copper, and
velvet, all vintage.

DRAMATIC
PSYCHEDELIA
Warm tones
for an outfit all in
orange and yellows
underscored in
vintage black, the
whole set off by
a more in-your-face
scarf (from H&M).

ETHNIC FOREVER
Audacious colors,
bold patterns,
and a necklace
found in a market.
You need to be tall
to carry this off.

His essentials

Eccentric doesn't have to mean kitsch. A single detail can
suffice: a colored frock coat over straight trousers and
black T-shirt, a fob watch, a colored Borsalino, red or zebra-
stripe shoes, or retro two-tones (avoid the commonplace
of trainers and go for Doc Martens instead), stripy or flowery waistcoats.

LAIRD CHIC
The explosive "tartan"
waistcoat by Vivienne
Westwood sends
a rather chilly colored
shirt into orbit; khaki
is here customized by
a packing ribbon from
Hermès, no less!

ROMANTIC

Your psychosocial profile

You go into ecstasies gazing at a Venetian sunset; a tear comes to your eye presented with a baby—or with a kiss at the movies, a Keats sonnet, a Chopin nocturne, or *Romeo and Juliet*.

You've always dreamed of wearing a Juliet gown complete with a train. Within you slumbers a Cinderella, a forlorn princess, an abandoned heroine. Your girly side makes you go gaga over Hello Kitty cashmere. You exude the kind of vulnerability that makes people want to take you under their wing. At home, your crimson curtains are held in place by tiebacks with droplets as elaborate as any baroque necklace.

In a boutique, you are irresistibly drawn to lace, to satin ribbons, to silk in black or pale pink. To make an impression at a soirée, you wax mysterious, proffering enigmatic remarks.

For your rendezvous in Paris, you choose the delicious Medici fountain in the Luxembourg Gardens; if in London, the heart of Hyde Park, aboard a rowboat on the Serpentine; or, in New York, a footbridge in Central Park overhung by a weeping willow like a languid, long-haired maiden.

FACING PAGE
CHIRP!
Clad in feathers and delicately floating satin ribbon, Vanessa Bruno's figure is all softness, at once vaporous and decidedly original.

LEFT
BAUDELAIRE THE DANDY
The inimitable nineteenth-century poet was also an astute observer of the looks and styles of his time.

Your icons

Poets, first and foremost, the Romantics or Baudelaire (never out of style), whose lovelorn lyricism you read today with undiminished ardor. Such sensitive souls often had an acute eye for the fashions of their time. In music, the inimitable Cole Porter. And today? The suave Molly Johnson.

IF YOU LIKE . . .

Your style

You love all things sensual, but don't go in for straight-up sexiness. Your femininity deals in nuances, in layers, in transparency. You adore long evening gowns? Go for it. Chiffon and underskirts, fluid, lightweight tops, diaphonous blouses. You can surf between revamped hippie and babydoll.

Your designers: Antik Batik, Isabelle Marant, Vanessa Bruno, Stella McCartney, Limi Feu (Yohji Yamamoto's daughter), Fifi Chachnil, and the Rodarte sisters.

Insolent stilettos are not your type. Opt for T-strap shoes or ballet flats. Yes to large brimmed soft hats and jewels in the hair. Snuggle up in soft cashmere or mohair (less expensive, just as warm). Rather than contrasts and geometry, go for shades of blush, blue, or black. Bordering on overload, you can't resist Liberty prints or flounces. Try to offset your namby-pamby side with some more modern accessories: flat boots, big, brightly colored bag, or a fitted jacket.

ROMANTIC

Her essentials

Printed lingerie, mildly retro lace slips, or an embroidered bodice unearthed in a market, cotton voile, Indian skirts and tunics. In winter, T-shirts with cardigans in fine or chunky knit. Ladylike handbags are not for you, so choose suede or aged leather. Beyond romanticism, your watchword should be softness.

Pure romantic refinement: Heschung shoes with floral-print uppers.

RED SUN
Beneath a tunic in silk chiffon (Mango), a silk shawl with flounces resembles a loincloth—all in shades of crimson.

BLUE LAKE
Over a 1950s vintage ball dress (or bridesmaid's dress?), a burgundy and old-rose mohair sweater.

AT THE MELANCHOLY BALL
A superfine knit sweater with a waterfall collar over a tulle underskirt: a complete black look enlivened by a velvet belt studded with gemstones.

WOODSTOCK ROMANTIC
Two tunics overlaid in a veil of vaporous and sexy chiffon embroidered Indian-style (Antik Batik).

ABOVE SUSPICION
A vintage dress (from a secondhand outlet, La Caverne à Fripes, in Montmartre), the waist set off by an immaculate wool crepe with nunnish, straight, loose pleats, brightened up by ivory and bronze-colored ribbons.

PAISLEY STREET
Delicate arabesques on vintage hippie pants with embroidered net top by Jean Paul Gaultier.

BLACK ROSE
That must-have romantic piece, the jabot shirt (Number Nine) worn under a Jean Paul Gaultier vest with ties, over classic pin-striped black trousers. The red flower is equally indispensible.

His essentials

Romanticism is not the sole prerogative of girls. There is room in the male wardrobe for a few flowery prints. Paul Smith lines shirt cuffs and collars with them. Dries Van Noten has imposed softer hues in menswear. The linchpins of male romanticism: ruffle-front shirts, recherché scarves, jewelry.

CLASSIC

Your psychosocial profile

For your graduation present, you asked your family to club together for a Hermès Kelly bag or a Chanel 2.55. You're still never without it. Moreover, you hate wasting money on things that might go out of fashion.

The couches in your lounge are in black or chocolate leather, the walls white or cream, the carpets Persian, and the curtains plain velvet. In Paris, you'd live in the sixteenth arrondissement (the storekeepers are so well brought-up there). You've taught your children (dressed in Petit Bateau, Ralph Lauren, or Zara) how to tidy their bedrooms. And, at the first sign of sun, all the family pulls on their Timberlands for a walk in the great outdoors. At a crowded party, you're slightly ill at ease as you can't decide whether you should help yourself at the buffet or wait until someone hands you a plate. On the whole, you'd prefer to dine at table. You note other people's extravagant getups with wry amusement, but you're quite happy in your little black dress or oxfords.

FACING PAGE
IDEAL BALANCE
Giorgio Armani has an infallible eye and a peerless sense of proportion, as can be seen in the timeless elegance of this suit.

LEFT
Catherine Deneuve: the very paragon of French chic.

Your icons

The *Mona Lisa* represents for you the acme of classical civilization, as much by her pose of reserve and sobriety as by the facture, perfect execution, delicate colors, studied composition, and at once serene and ambiguous atmosphere created by Leonardo at the peak of his powers. If you had a present-day hero it might well be the Queen of England, though you have a weakness for the timeless understatement of her daughter, Princess Anne.

Your style

For you Chanel remains the acme of style. If
you don't invariably appreciate the updated
version peddled by Karl Lagerfeld, you have
to concede that his finishes are always
impeccable. When you need a smart outfit
you instinctively head for a suit (Saint
Laurent or Renoma rather than Courrèges
or Moschino). You remain fully wedded to
the timeless elegance of the little black
dress. With white collar and cuffs? Why
not? It's different. Come spring, you swap
somber hues for two-tone navy and white
in the best taste. Both spruce and feminine.
Your classics go through season after season without tiring: your twinsets, your black
skirts, your Burberry, your Ralph Lauren peacoat, your Cartier watch. One is never passé
in classics.

Fluorescent colors are not your cup of tea.
The brightest you manage is Hermès
orange—apart from the packaging of your
Brides de Gala headscarf. Hermès, that's
another of your darlings, you love it for the
quality of its materials (a soft spot of yours),
and its unbeatably supple leather jackets. As
you privilege elegant comfort above all, you
are not one to struggle into spray-on jeans.
You know what your assets are, and to show
off your bust, you pin a vintage pearl brooch
on your Diane Von Furstenberg wrap dress.
You have not fallen for the vogue for harem
pants, even from Céline: hardly becoming,
though nobody dares say so. And you don't
think much of the trikini by Eres either. The
very idea! To cut bits out of a perfectly good
one-piece! On the other hand, you did snap
up one little extravagance: a sequined Breton
shirt. Navy blue and white.

CLASSIC

Her essentials

Your basics are not overwhelmingly inventive, but they do last: Chanel two-tone pumps with contrasting heel and toe (best in beige and black) go with everything, be it to lunch or dinner. A black wool fitted jacket by Sonia Rykiel or Armani goes over 501s, pleated Cerruti trousers, or a Zara skirt. One doesn't have to spend a fortune to be well turned-out: V-neck sweaters by Uniqlo, like their down jackets, prove excellent value. Lastly, the inevitable white shirt—from Gap or A.P.C.—has pride of place in your closet.

VERSAILLES
RIVE GAUCHE
A simple shirtwaist
dress, here in spruce-
green plaid (Zara),
brightened up
by a cascade of
pearls à la Chanel.

CLASSIC LINES
Dark blue satin
with a beautiful
deep violine with
decorative seams:
a dress from H&M.
As for the red
cashmere, today
it's almost become
a classic.

HOTEL PIERRE
The eternal twinset
adorned with
a vintage pearl
necklace and the
equally perennial
pencil skirt (Mango).
Classicism with
stilettos that never
goes out of style.

SAND AND WIND
For a stroll in the spray, a striped Breton top personalized by ruffled white collar, with a raincoat made snugger by a gentleman's scarf. The jeans, of course, are unfussy straight-legs (Uniqlo).

TENNIS WHITES
Cool lines set against an off-white jacket (Calvin Klein). Such immutable pin-striped pants are fit for any season (Bill Tornade).

EVENING PLEATS
Just one of the innumerable versions of the little black dress. Here, by Chanel—but more affordable ones exist and they are just as chic. Colored tights add a more contemporary and imaginative touch.

GRAY CLASS
Classic, yes, but here it's a Mugler. Close-fitting, inverted lapel notches: only the experienced eye notices. Tie or no, as you fancy.

His essentials

The two-piece suit—neither too wide, nor too narrow—no longer has to be worn with a necktie to be classic. On the other hand, there's no room for error with the shirt: banish the large-spread Italian collar, as well as any of a different color from the shirt. Go for one color (camel, tobacco, bronze, purple, gray, charcoal gray, pearl; in general Olivier Strelli pulls these off well) that will make a change from your eternal black V-neck and striped shirt. Leather and suede are fine by you, but more in a fur-lined or safari jacket or a parka than in a short windbreaker. Your labels are the same as for the female of the species, with the addition of Celio for inexpensive cashmeres, Adolfo Dominguez for sleek coats and shirts, Old England for lodens, and Costume National for a dash of originality. Banish tasseled loafers forever, and opt for Westons or their copies. If you like a blazer, choose it well: neither too short, nor overlong, it should sit on the shoulders, the buttons not too shiny.

SPORTY

Your psychosocial profile

Your favorite walk on Saturday afternoons when you've finished exercising (working out, judo, Pilates, lengths in the pool) is to Citadium (behind Printemps Haussmann in Paris), to Adidas (Original Store in Berlin), to the Niketown (in New York). Or to Decathlon (everywhere). The diversity of sports fashion has to be seen to be believed. If you are uncompromising about your go-to labels, you are on the other hand rather less choosy about your cosmetics, since there are some excellent ones to be had in supermarkets.

Your light-filled loft furnished from Ikea has a shelf with a gold cup for motocross, a hiking stick, and a medal you got skydiving. On one of your white walls you've pinned a painting of a forest that looks as real as a photo and a cool poster of an Australian surfer catching a tube. You have a Japanese futon instead of a bed and two others as couches that you unroll for your friends for your crack-of-dawn departures. You never miss a film on sports or on nature, and set your alarm clock religiously for four in the morning so as to watch the Olympics live on TV. Of course, you watch your diet, you've got rid of all cow's milk dairy products, take vitamin C every day, but you don't mind a glass of fine Bordeaux—there's no point going overboard. You're not a nun after all and like to have fun. You like your clothes and are a sucker for cake. In any event, you work off any flab mornings on your Airex gym mat, which you keep rolled up in a corner.

FACING PAGE
SIMPLE CASHMERE Tommy Hilfiger here adopts Hamptons casual-smart, an easy-to-wear style of which his customers are particularly fond.

LEFT
TAKE THAT! An intense Hilary Swank in Clint Eastwood's *Million Dollar Baby*.

Your icons

In addition to the inevitable sports stars—some under contract with major labels—your expert eye knows how to appreciate the sculpted physiques of certain kings and queens of showbiz: you're impressed by Madonna, by Hilary Swank for her breathtaking performance in *Million Dollar Baby* where she plays a woman boxer and that indestructible champion of the workout, Sigourney Weaver.

Your style

That little floral number is not for you. You're more jeans, leggings, sweatsuits. Sports brands are diversifying their style. It's high time. The days of flashy leotards, Rocky Balboa jogging tops, and shapeless T-shirts are over. From Nike to Reebok, from Adidas, Puma, Tacchini, Quicksilver, to Repetto, Bloch (dance), not forgetting rapper brands (see pages 90–93, Fashion, Street and Rock) and ready-to-wear labels like Lacoste and Tommy Hilfiger, sportswear has become streetwear. Now, even top designers go in for sport collections: technical materials, topstitching to bring out the physique, contrasting piping, pockets galore, Marithé + François Girbaud, Gaultier, Versace. You prefer Adidas for their more feminine lines and for their collaboration with Yohji Yamamoto. You broke the bank for a Y3 and an Eagle. You dispose, moreover, of an impressive array of running shoes, almost a different pair for every outfit: high-tops with trousers, lower and lighter (so as not to "shorten" the leg) with shorts, Bermudas, or pedal pushers. And a collection of denim jackets (Girbaud when you have the cash): fitted, square-shouldered, topstitched, with panels and pleats, vintage, and in every shade of blue, even if the rumor about the phoniness of allegedly organic denim shocks your green sensibility. You also possess a dazzling spectrum of close-fitting T-shirts that you wear one over the other in varying colors or tones and densities, while shoulder-straps and hems play peekaboo. If you're slender, the sky's the limit: long, cropped, low-cut, whatever. If you are curvy, slip on a shirt or tunic, or tie a cardigan round your hips. Don't make the mistake of dressing up in total athletic wear or top-to-toe denim: team a feminine Isabelle Marant, Esprit, or Zara top with your Levi's or a white Calvin Klein shirt with your Ecko or Repetto leggings.

SPORTY

Her essentials

Uniqlo is your Mecca. Their accessibly priced jeans, shirts, sweaters, and T-shirts in natural fabrics in every color make for a sporty look of a thousand facets, from the droll to the discreet: try total fuchsia or midnight blue punctuated with burgundy. American Apparel occupies the same niche, but upmarket. Technical research undertaken by major brands has resulted in some real comfort pluses. As to style, Adidas and Reebok rule your roost. Your must-haves: track jacket, Converse, fleece blouson, and, for the cyclist, why not one by Jean Paul Gaultier, beneath a bodysuit or a Repetto wrap top?

BASQUIAT ATHLETIC
Graffiti inspired by
the painter printed
on Reebok high-tops.

OLYMPIC LEOPARD
Cycle shorts (Reebok)
don't preclude sex
appeal, at least not if
they are teamed with
leopard-print top and
a man's striped shirt
(Calvin Klein Jeans).

A LITTLE JOGGING
ON THE PRAIRIE
All in green for
Yamamoto–Adidas
jogging pants and
Reebok tank top,
warmed by some
vintage cashmere
Leonard.

FROM FISHING
TO SOCCER
Rolled-up
comfortable cords
(H&M) under an old-
school Adidas jacket,
given a feminine
touch with jewelry
for a night
out clubbing.

THE FRENCH OPEN
Over a classic tennis
mini-dress (Reebok),
a long top in silk
chiffon (Zara).

MATCH POINT
Bold contrast
between the
turquoise Reebok
mini and the sheer
bright red top
and ribbed knit.

SPORTY NIGHTLIFE
See-through pink
camisole with a
black ensemble:
Reebok jogging
pants sporting wide
satin piping and
faux leather hoodie
(American Apparel).

IN THE WOODS
In an Yves Saint
Laurent tweed
jacket and Marithé
+ François Girbaud
jeans, a neat
balance between
smart and relaxed.

His essentials

Resist the desire to show off your muscles. Admittedly, a baggy T-shirt
with overlarge sleeves is a heresy, but a skintight jersey over the pecs
(or a budding pair of love handles) is just not flattering. Today, there's no
excuse for badly fitting menswear. Overlay fluorescent or bright prints
on top of plain colors. The polo shirt is a stalwart, but it lacks originality—
even a Lacoste. Go for unusual necklines: concealed buttons, zippers,
snaps. As for the full track suit: to be worn with caution if you don't want
to look like a 50 Cent clone.

SOPHISTICATED

Your psychosocial profile

Always perfect from top to toe, you can't imagine leaving the house without manicured nails. You adore furniture from the 1940s and 1950s and gorgeous textiles. You are often asked for advice in organizing parties because you have a nose for refined detail. You have a knack for arriving at a "couture" style with vintage clothes, and not necessarily spending a fortune. You are a mine of information on the most recent catwalk shows (you watch them on style.com) and on the merits of the new Mulberry datebook as compared to a Filofax. You adore entertaining and going out, to friends' places or restaurants, and you hone in on the most select bars, trendsetting bistros, and easygoing (at last) Japanese eateries before any one else. Places with unforgiving lighting are shunned. You can spend a sleepless night because you're not sure what to wear the next day—or in two days or in a week—or what to put in your bag for the long weekend two months away. For you, cultivating your style is a full-time job that's as demanding as tending the gardens at Versailles.

FACING PAGE
ERUDITE
ASYMMETRY
The originality
of Paul Smith
stripes.

LEFT
GLAMOUR AND
THEN SOME!
Lauren Bacall
in the studied
simplicity of
a dress with
draped bust
underscored
in black, but
no necklace.
Pure 1940s,
in cascading
waves, sensual,
refined.

Your icons

You adore Dita Von Teese for her impeccable and original style that cocks a snook at fashion. You love American films of the 1950s so much you could watch them with the sound turned down because the sets and costumes alone are a feast for the eyes. No one will ever be as chic as Lauren Bacall, Gene Tierney, Gloria Swanson, Cary Grant, Clark Gable, and Spencer Tracy. In Europe, beautiful Italian stars of ages past fire your imagination: Sophia Loren, Silvana Mangano, Monica Vitti. And you'd watch *The Umbrellas of Cherbourg* over and over for its shimmering colors. You confess you rather enjoyed Sarah Jessica Parker's extravagant frocks in the movie version of *Sex and the City*, but you can't stand how slovenly TV presenters have become and deplore the abandonment of dress codes at the theater and for dinner.

Your style

Resolutely feminine, you revel in retro suits
and will wear a tight (but not short) skirt by
Alaïa with a 1950s fitted jacket and stiletto
heels. Shoes train the posture and therefore
the bearing: you like the curve in your back
produced by a good pair of pumps. You are
ready to splash out on a pair of Pradas,
Walter Steigers, or Diors. If you're short of
cash, you know all the good bargain designer
outlets. It's the same thing for bags. And you
have an eye for the way a fabric falls, a sure
sign of quality. Your favorite materials are all
the most chic: duchesse satin for its density
and sheen, velvet (silk, preferably), wool crepe
for its mattness, thick jersey for its hold. You
are a maniac when it comes to jacket arm
holes that should mold the shoulder and arm
without bunching.

You've been seen wearing slacks but seldom jeans, too casual. You seem always to
have known the shape that suits you—
straight or cigarette line, preferably with a
front crease. Joseph is a favorite, and Saint
Laurent, but you can also find something to
enjoy in Zara or Mango. You'll change the buttons on a coat or jacket to add refinement—
especially if it's emblazoned with an outsized
logo. What a total lack of style! That's why
you loathe Vuitton fabric and bags stamped
with the letters D.i.o.r in glitzy metal. A tiny red
"Chanel," on the other hand, is not displeasing.
But, in general, you steer clear of it bags. You
possess ten black dresses, but you also like
color—though you never mix more than two
tones—fur, leopard prints, and you wouldn't
be seen dead without jewelry and gloves. As
you know only too well your figure's weak
points, you don't waste days of your life tramp-
ing around the stores. If you are slim, you'll go
for vintage or find just the right dress at Cardin,
Courrèges, Chloé, or Paule Ka. If you're tall, then
it's Dries Van Noten, Marni, and Sonia Rykiel.
Minor brands are not your style: too common,
too often copied.

SOPHISTICATED

Her essentials

As you're not some starlet ignorant of the rudiments of fashion and dressed by a couture house, you know full well that accessories can be enough to glamorize a style: shoes, bag, and gloves first, then a hat—or veil—belt, and jewelry. Some experienced Parisians are able to upgrade their daywear for evening. A pair of spectacular or stylish earrings will suffice. Or long gloves. The timeless black sheath dress remains a sure bet, as do foundation and scarlet lipstick.

STYLISH LACE
Vintage Christian
Lacroix dress that
sums up the whole
style of this talented
couturier: the
juxtaposition
of lace with
wide honey and
eggplant stripes.

SMART ATTITUDE
The skirt
(vintage Armani)
features a very fine
lurex thread, the
sleeveless Mariot
Chanet top is in
wool lace, the jacket
(Lacroix) hints at
a tux but is fitted.

BEIGE BEIGE
AND TULLE
The putty-colored
tutu dress (Mango)
is brightened up
by a huge necklace
(Mango), while the
jacket (Top Shop)
boasts a very
"couture" flouncy
ruched neckline.

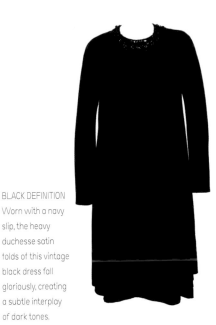

BLACK DEFINITION
Worn with a navy
slip, the heavy
duchesse satin
folds of this vintage
black dress fall
gloriously, creating
a subtle interplay
of dark tones.

WINGED DAMSEL
On a dragonfly-
hemmed vintage
Rochas ensemble,
a daringly kitsch
ivy-green ceramic
necklace (vintage
Burma jewelry).

GARMISCH–
PARTENKIRCHEN
Hippie jacket
(Antik Batik)
contrasts with
a delicate chiffon skirt
(Alberta Ferretti).

His essentials

Sophistication is to be found in the details: the socks, for example, must
imperatively be the same color as the shoes or trousers. No, you don't
have to match shoes and pants: a pair of ocher suede Paul Smiths goes
perfectly with the all-over black or navy look. Moreover, for the most
part, suede is more distinctive than leather. Train your eye to spot
nuances in color: sky-blue should not make you look like a civil servant.
Khaki should not be allowed to "jaundice" the complexion. Don't fall into
the all-cashmere trap: a merino turtleneck is suppler than your average
cashmere and pills less. As the goal is to sculpt your silhouette and
smooth over its defects; avoid a down jacket that might turn you into
a Pillsbury doughboy. Adolfo Dominguez and Armani bring out the best
in you. In summer, prefer predominant beige tones, so much smarter
than white. If you are getting a bit of a paunch, wear your linen, cotton,
microfiber, heavy silk—over pleated pants (always elegant).

EAT IT UP
An imaginative touch.
The Dior jacket with
intricate buttons
unexpectedly
joins twill pants.
Underneath: Fine
jersey T-shirt with
open V-neck (Armani).

ABSOLUTELY ARTY

Your psychosocial profile

Whether you're walking along the Thames Path in London, standing in line at Berthillon's (the *glacier* on the Île Saint-Louis in Paris), demonstrating in support of illegal immigrants, or looking over a squat in a disused suburban factory, your eye acts like a camera, filming, recording the landscape. You just can't help it: you see performance art everywhere. A sour-faced supermarket cashier out on her feet, a beggar in the subway, a child howling in the sandpit, a couple fighting over dinner—for you everything offers an opportunity to meditate on the aesthetic aspects of life. And, when your boy- or girlfriend dumps you, you look at yourself crying in the mirror and think you look like a Nan Goldin.

In a restaurant, even if it means paying through the nose, you'll order a mineral water because of the design of the bottle. Leaving your home in the evening, your guests suffer from minor backache thanks to your designer chairs. They haven't eaten much either, since their tastebuds were confused by your hundred percent yellow dinner. Your children are sometimes entitled to a McDonald's simply because your eye is attuned to the Formica lines of the decor. You arrive with concept gifts at birthday parties: a beautiful dead leaf, a pair of handcuffs, or a cola nut imported from Mali.

BELOW
OH PEGGY!
The American
Peggy Guggenheim
(1898–1979),
a major collector of modern art, gallery owner, and patron, was literally an "art addict"; she said so herself. Marcel Duchamp and Jean Cocteau gave her some pointers, but this original, amusing, and free-and-easy grande dame honed her tastes on her own. During the Nazi occupation of France, her exceptional collection of masterpieces was hidden away in the museum at Grenoble. She brought dozens of great artists to prominence, saved many Jews, had many lovers, and married (among others) Max Ernst. In addition to the Guggenheim Collection in New York, she left the sublime Palazzo dei Leoni in Venice, where she died, as a museum.

Your icons

You are always first in line to a new museum opening anywhere in the world. From Quai Branly in Paris to the Punta della Dogana in Venice, not to mention all the Guggenheims, you go into ecstasies about installations that you alone understand. Cindy Sherman and her disguises delight you, Takashi Murakami and the sweet little faces of his hilarious mangas send you into raptures. You meditate on Damien Hirst's radical statements and you dream of a dress with Daniel Buren stripes. Biopics of painters and sculptors are your idea of an evening at the movies and you'll save for years to afford a sublime vintage print by Man Ray.

FACING PAGE
ORIGAMI
The widely admired English designer Gareth Pugh's catwalk shows are as much art performances as presentations of clothing. Here, a very *Star Trek* model from summer 2009. (He does create more customer-friendly attire.)

Your style

Choose clothing that shows off this arty side. Novel textures, graphic patterns inspired by artworks, handpainted dresses, craft pieces, jewelry, unique accessories whose designer's name you can quote with pride. Show an interest in novel textures like the neoprene jackets of Élisabeth de Senneville, origami T-shirts by Mashallah. Design, 3-D dresses by the Korean Lie Sang Bong, and of course the shimmering folded "Fortuny" of Issey Miyake (whose Pleats Please collection is more afford-able). Unearthing fledgling designers is part and parcel of the game. Try to attend gradua-tion shows at Studio Berçot in Paris, Central Saint Martins in London, or Parsons in New York. The hairdresser is for trimming your geo-metric or asymmetric square cut, your bowl cut, or shaving half your skull—a look enhanced by tattoos and sophisticated makeup.

As to designers, you can quietly ruin yourself for a Martin Margiela or Yohji Yamamoto jacket (you say "Yohji") because they're col-lector's items. You sport Doc Martens with graffiti (and signatures) or the almost-impos-sible-to-find futuristic stilts of Alexander McQueen's last show. As you are prepared to undergo any torture in order to maximize your look, you keep a close eye on H&M's (very) lim-ited designer collections, standing in line at six in the morning in the freezing cold. Viktor & Rolf, Matthew Williamson, and Comme des Garçons (shortened to "Comme des") hang in glory in your wardrobe. Not one for the canons of traditional elegance, you are prepared to wear almost anything as long as the ensem-ble makes artistic sense.

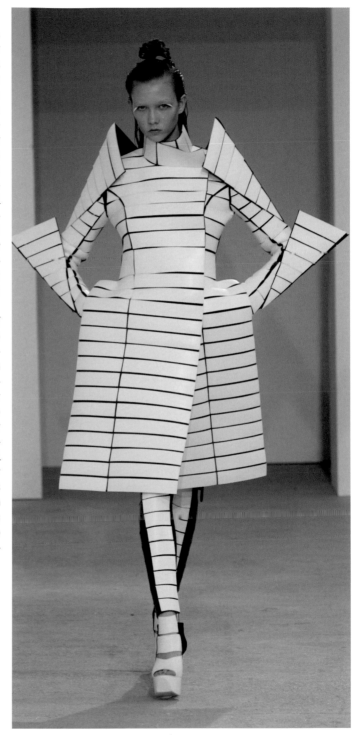

Her essentials

Shirts and knits by the Belgian Ann Demeulemeester are splendidly minimalistic. Certain pieces by agnès b. boast graffiti, artists' drawings, or a streak of paint applied by hand. Do you like printed T-shirts bristling with references? There's pop art by the Belgian Walter Van Beirendonck, and philosophy, as with Castelbajac ("Too strange to live, too rare to die" or "Thank God I'm an atheist"). The arty ideal: print up original drawings yourself (everywhere on the Internet).

CORRIDA PABLO
Optical games form an integral part of your style. Here, a Top Shop sweater over a vintage skirt.

MATISSE COLORS

You have no hesitation in running roughshod over the conventions of color "matching" and juxtaposing those that initially appear incompatible. Here, a harmony between a burgundy Yohji Yamamoto jacket and a vermilion Alaïa skirt, linked by a loose purple blouse.

SEURAT ONLINE

Be brave and combine stripes (vintage Yves Saint Laurent) with a more impressionistic piece of fabric tied into a skirt.

MONDRIAN BLACK

Vintage skirt with "cobweb print" and vintage Paule Ka twinset.

DELAUNAY GRAPHICS
The Anne Valérie Hash jacket is made of a high-tech fabric resembling pasteboard manufactured in Sankt Gallen, Switzerland, by the firm of Jakob Schlaepfer. The effect is softened with a printed silk skirt (Comme des Garçons).

FAUVIST RAINBOW
A range of purples for this tulle jacket by Anne Valérie Hash in dilute tones worn with agnès b. satin pants. The necklace by Pellini weighs more than a pound, but one has to suffer to be beautiful.

POLLOCK, MARK TWO
Glinting like gemstones, the print on this silk dress by Peter Pilotto makes it shimmer in the evening light. The structured jacket is Japanese (5351 Pour Les Femmes).

GRAY CHECK
An eccentric, arty version of the suit: the spencer-cum-double-breasted jacket hybrid is by Hedi Slimane for Dior Homme; worn with a shirt but no tie and slim check Number Nine pants. The death's-head pin is by Marie Besançon.

His essentials

For a man, the merest screen-printed T-shirt can be enough to give you an arty touch. Avoid the temptation of the hackneyed "Born to Kill" or "Fuck"—not very experimental slogans (unless it's signed Ben). Designers like Paul Smith and Dries Van Noten combine color and print for a understated outsider look. Rick Owens has reinvented classics with drape and the sobriety of bias cut. Go for artist or designer customized trainers and shoes. Finally it's best to eschew baroque or kitsch overkill—cute for girls, riskier for boys.

ULTRASEXY

Your psychosocial profile

When you come in, the temperature goes up. Is it your sashay, your gaze, your way of lighting a cigarette—of asking for a light—your clothes? Or all of the above? What is undeniable is that such splendid feminine assurance tends to get up the nose of your fellow women. Instinctively, you weave sensual complicities. You flirt, subtly. Moreover, you acknowledge the fact: evenings devoid of this savor of seduction bore you. Your apartment resembles you: hot colors, dimmer switches, and deep sofas. On the walls, sexy pop lithographs by Tom Wesselmann and the colorful sensuality of Jacques Bosser. On your mantelpiece: a figurine of Betty Boop. Your favorite music? Billie Holiday, Sade, Harry Belafonte for the warm caress of their voices. You've tried a pole-dancing class and acquired a sex toy by Sonia Rykiel. You have little taste for raves in improbable and poorly heated venues, preferring more elaborate and convivial soirées. Fond of your food, lunch calls for good bread, and you boycott restaurants whose nouvelle cuisine portions mean you need a pizza afterward. You could break the bank for pretty lingerie. In fact you do. Often.

FACING PAGE
UNDRESS ME!
Jean Paul Gaultier is the champion of the erotic whose codes he shakes and shuffles, as much for men as for women. Here we have a mix of Juliette Greco and Berlin cabaret.

LEFT
SWING HIGH!
Marilyn was at once fresh, innocent, and sultry. A blonde bombshell.

Your icons

Your leanings are retro: Marilyn Monroe—her curves, her irresistible smile, her touching insecurity—embodies for you the acme of endearing femininity, while Marlon Brando is the epitome of male sensuality. In Europe, the daring actress Romy Schneider and the magnetic allure of Alain Delon remain unbeatable. In another genre, you love watching the disconcerting Charlotte Rampling in *The Night Porter*.

Your style

Sex appeal is a state of mind rather a question of dress. You have to know, and look after, your strong points. Not just breasts and bottom: glossy skin, beautiful hair, lovely hands, shapely legs, a pretty neck, even a hint of androgyny. You can indulge in the classic plunging V-necked cashmere or the insolence of an Alaïa dress whose cut could eroticize anyone's figure. Xuly Bët, less expensive, gets rid of the hang-ups of the fat and the lean with close-hugging lines in lycra, plain or with graffiti. But you can also play on the ambiguity of a straight or bias-cut dress in sheer silk by Adeline André, whose airy buoyancy hints at the naked body beneath. Don't restrict yourself to black chiffon: try overlaying the sublimely colored variants by the Indian Rajesh Pratap Singh. If you can go bra-less, expose your back at every conceivable opportunity.

For you, the leopard print is a basic, on a retro coat, on shoes, bags, a flimsy, ruffle-front blouse or buttoned to the throat (above all *not* a vulgar spray-on bodystocking). Leather or python blouson, close-fitting dress, or bolero (from Alaïa or Jean-Claude Jitrois) impart that indispensible animal touch. Avoid slacks in stretch leather, vinyl, lycra—fun perhaps, but seldom flattering. Lastly, don't forget all that lingerie can do: a lacy slip worn under a jacket or a loose sweater, satin bra in a contrasting color under a blouse with the buttons half-undone, seamed stockings and garter-belt, long-line bustier (by Vivienne Westwood) slipped into trousers or jeans, push-up waspie. In addition to Alaïa, every other season designers dream up variants on the sexy theme. For Jean Paul Gaultier, it is a relaxed, liberated woman in a slashed dress exposing the skin, straps that remold the body, fishnets, printed tattoos, satin bras. For Barbara Bui, a rock queen in black, figure-hugging, sprayed, studded, or bespangled pants. For Dolce & Gabbana, a Mediterranean pinup.

ULTRASEXY

Her essentials

Never be without stiletto heels that flex the back. Try platform soles to lengthen the leg or flats if your ankles are slender. Long-line and half-cup bras (padded, perhaps) show off your bust to best advantage: Etam, Victoria's Secret, Aubade, Chantelle, Chantal Thomass, Fifi Chachnil, and Agent Provocateur are the sexiest labels. You need a pencil skirt (split or no) to show off your hips. And a trenchcoat to play Marilyn, or the shiny black version, why not? Finally, never neglect perfume: flowery, amber, or vanilla.

IF YOU LIKE . . .

DESIRES OF THE FLESH
A "nude" satin body by
Sonia Rykiel for H&M
adds sexiness to the
lines of a gent's tuxedo
pants belted with a tie.

ROSE-TINTED
Silk bandeau
bra for small busts
(Rykiel for H&M),
worn beneath an
ultrafine lace blouse
over a gathered
two-layer chiffon
skirt (Alberta
Ferretti).

BEIJING BLACK
All very *In the Mood
for Love*, Chinese
dresses throw
everyone's libido
into a tizzy.

SUN ROCK
A denim jacket left
open to reveal a bra
in contrasting color
is as effective as
any plunging
neckline. The same
can be said of the
scarf draped over
the hips like a skirt.

HOT SAND
Figure-hugging
dress in two-tone
net and "crumpled"
blouse: sexy meets
arty.

HIDE-AND-SEEK
Superfine viscose
jersey sweater
(Alberta Ferretti)
worn without bra
and toned down
(if that's the term!)
by a skintight
knee-length skirt.

HAWAIIAN GIGOLO
Over rippling
bronzed abs, a
vintage bejeweled
vest adorned with
Lesage embroidery
and offset by (mock)
"lost generation"
jeans. The jeans
here are customized
with motifs cut
out of 1950s
curtain material.
Then there's the
goth necklace by
Marie Besançon.

His essentials

Since Hedi Slimane came up with a slim-fitting suit for Dior Homme, male
bodies can be exposed and exploded. Buttock-hugging pants are worn
wide or narrow. If you go for baggies, don't forget designer boxers that
should peep over your impeccable abs. Avoid shorts (run-of-the-mill) and
opt for Bermudas, with a vest with nothing underneath, for instance.
Something more discreet? Soft, diaphanous materials, such as cashmere,
fine cotton, fishnet. Jewelry—in gray and matt metal, or diamond, but
understated—draw the eye to your fine hands and exfoliated skin. A word
to the wise though: for a shaven head you'll need a perfect profile. If not,
hair worn long but neat gives that essential sensual touch. Among the
fashion houses that indulge male sex appeal are Versace, Dolce & Gabbana,
Jean Paul Gaultier, and Gareth Pugh, who have each succeeded in renewing our idea of virility, and . . . Zara.

BAROQUE
An intriguing
Philippe Ferrandis
necklace recalls
old-style rivers
of pearls and
brooches, all the
while managing
to look eminently
contemporary.

3

Fashion has an impact on everything, from the silver screen to engineering. No film, no play sees the light of day vvithout a costume director. No singer or pop group can make it vvithout carefully planning their look. In sports, in space exploration, from tailored suits to svvimsuits, from vvindbreakers to undergarments, fashion and technology advance hand in hand. The ongoing collaboration betvveen art and fashion is timeless. As for its various sociological signifiers, the interface betvveen vvorld events and style trends is all-pervasive.

FASHION AND THE MOVIES

Actresses and actors readily confess that it's when they go for their first costume fitting that they really begin to get under the skin of a character. The costume director explains: "You have to make the fabric speak, so that the costume, too, becomes an actor, that every accessory has a meaning." She spends hours defining the roles and looking for prototypes to copy that are refined in the course of endless adjustments. She sees how an actress can be transfigured by a dress, and has plenty of anecdotes about attacks of nerves in front of the mirror.

Fashion serves here to transmogrify. It's not really dress for daywear, or work, or evening: it sets the scene.

An accessory or a clever combination can be enough to make a costume "speak." Some actresses made their name thanks to a dress: the voluptuous Mae West in *I'm No Angel* or Judy Garland in *A Star is Born*, not to mention Audrey Hepburn, on whom it was the cinema that bestowed a fashion dimension. It was for *Sabrina*, shot in 1954 by Billy Wilder, that she first asked to be dressed by Hubert de Givenchy. The effect was unforgettable: Givenchy found this ravishing clotheshorse (exceptionally slim for the time) to be a magnificent muse. Hepburn herself was to demand Givenchy for all her subsequent movies. In exchange, her distinction and grace was enriched by genuine Parisian chic that transformed the star into a fashion icon, a status only enhanced by her role in *Funny Face* (1957) by Stanley Donen, a delicious musical on fashion in which she dances with Fred Astaire. Above and beyond all the froth, the film abounds in aperçus of the fashion photographer's trade. Fred Astaire's character was inspired by Richard Avedon, one of the first to dare to photograph models out of the studio, for *Harper's Bazaar*. It shows the equivalents of today's touching-up or airbrushing, as well as the artificiality of the poses typical of those years. Visually, the film boasts a gloriously harmonious color scheme, which remains a treasure trove for screenwriters and couturiers alike.

Over time, movies touching on the world of fashion became more and more documentary. Hovering between cynicism and humor William Klein's *Who Are You, Polly Magoo?* (1966) is a fabulous portrait of the delirious 1960s and of the fashion

AUDREY HEPBURN
The very first fashion star, an actress sculpted like a Tanagra figurine and infatuated with the talent of her friend, the designer Hubert de Givenchy. Here in a timeless black sheath dress, long gloves, 1960s necklace, earrings, and diadem, in *Breakfast at Tiffany's*, naturally.

milieu. Forty years later, the same qualities explain the huge success of *The Devil Wears Prada* by David Frankel (2006). Meryl Streep and her amazing designer garb were much admired. But it was also fun to be a fly on the wall in the offices of a "real" glossy monthly. The script might sometimes have verged on caricature but the characters encapsulate an era both showy and pitiless. In response to this blockbuster's worldwide success, a real-life documentary on American *Vogue* entitled *The September Issue* went on general release to great acclaim.

The world of fashion is a goldmine for moviemakers. Robert Altman's *Prêt-à-Porter* (1994) paints a savage portrait behind the scenes at the Paris catwalk that culminates in a murder. Grandstanding egos, spiteful putdowns, backstage backstabbing, panic among the designers before the curtain goes up, hysterical outbursts from the stars at the shows. All these ingredients make for two hours twenty minutes of caustic satire. The team shot some scenes live at the collections and garnered much valuable information from Sonia and Nathalie Rykiel. Of course, the fashionistas—columnists and stylists alike—were delighted and outraged in equal measure.

Jean Paul Gaultier recounts that it was seeing *Falbalas* as a child that made him decide to become a fashion designer. Made in 1944 by Jacques Becker (with Micheline Presle), the film (entitled *Paris Frills* in English) is a tragic story of love and treason against the backdrop of life in a couture house. In defiance of war restrictions, the production boasts sublime gowns by Marcel Rochas—a benchmark—and hats by Gabrielle, soon to be Coco, Chanel. If one revels in the grandiose sets (Max Douy) and dazzling costumes, as much as in the stilted dialogue and luxuriously quaint furnishings, the film also serves as a historic document.

In short, like dance, boxing, or the police, the world of fashion is as "cinegenic" as it is sociologically revealing.

AND GOD CREATED BARDOT
In 1956, the movie *And God Created Woman* by Roger Vadim propelled Brigitte Bardot to the rank of international star and sex symbol, and the incarnation of female emancipation. She plays a girl who is both paragon and she-devil, guileless yet provocative, fancy- and carefree, inspiring idolatry and indignation in equal measure. She also popularized

plunge-neck leotards, full-skirted dresses, capri pants, and ballet flats.

FACING PAGE
OUT ON THE RED CARPET
Sarah Jessica Parker (alias Carrie Bradshaw), star of *Sex and the City* has, since 1998 (in the USA) and 2000 (in France), become the most in-demand fashion icon of our era. Here, in Chanel haute couture, at the Emmy Awards in Los Angeles.

FASHION AND ART

From the very beginnings of haute couture, fashion has flirted with artists: art nouveau, surrealism, Dada, cubism, abstraction. From Elsa Schiaparelli (whose lobster dress was emblazoned with a huge drawing by Dali, crayfish buttons, drawer-pockets, the hat-cum-pumps) to Yves Saint Laurent (with the Mondrian dress, the cape with guitars inspired by Braque, the dress with doves inspired by Matisse), without forgetting Sonia Delaunay's fabrics, fashion is not only fed by the designer's inspiration, their imagination also borrows from painters. Art and fashion, however, don't function at the same tempo. Art aims to last, while fashion, well, drops out of fashion. However fleetingly, it also has to factor in human morphology. Thus, a garment can never hope to be a completely free work; it can only strive to become one.

In the 1980s, Japanese designers embarked on daring stylistic experimentation in the shape of the "concept" cut: oversized and asymmetrical, with triple sleeves and haphazard button placings. Interestingly, all of them, from Comme des Garçons to Yohji Yamamoto, have reverted to more conventional lines for the sake of the business. Fashion is not art, and Lacroix, Gaultier, and Lagerfeld know this full well. Nevertheless, some catwalks verge on a happening: when the late Alexander McQueen sent an amputee model down the runway wearing prosthetic legs or when he had robots squirt colored paint on to white dresses, his position was as radical as any artistic statement. For many, his later, gentler, more poetic shows remain pure moments of creativity. And he is not the only one whose shows elicit from its audience emotions as highly charged as any opera.

LINES, JUST LINES
The famous Mondrian dress in jersey, designed by Yves Saint Laurent in 1965.

FACING PAGE
Hermès regularly purchases sketches by contemporary artists to illustrate its famous silk scarves, issuing them in a limited edition of 200. Here, the Bauhaus artist Josef Albers.

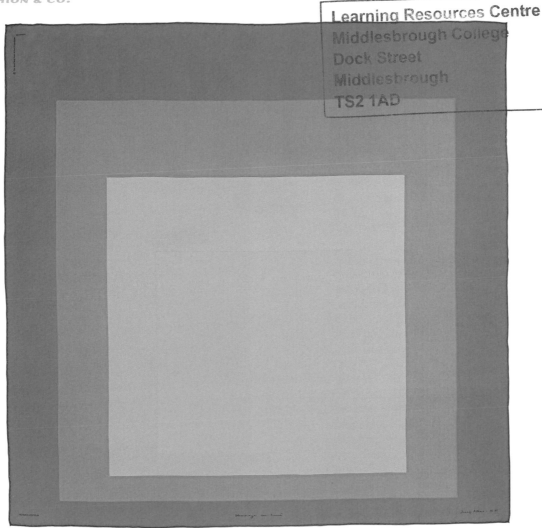

Artistic or not, it has to be admitted that, in the frenzy of a seasonal rhythm that demands incessant innovation, fashion is blowing itself out, losing its very substance. In the quest for "meaning," some fashion houses take on artists so as to give their products the "weight" of a referent.

Hermès has, for example, printed a limited series of two hundred silk squares reproducing fabrics by Josef Albers. The scarf was sold in a special box, accompanied by a brochure with details about the artist. Since 2003, Vuitton has collaborated with Japanese artist Takashi Murakami to give new life and an arty spin to its canvas fabric bags: these manga models have been pretty successful and Murakami earned a worldwide reputation, as well as a retrospective at the Guggenheim Museum in Bilbao (in 2009) sponsored by … Vuitton. Both sides reap the benefit. Murakami is no Soulages or Pollock, and

Vuitton judged rightly that this tongue-in-cheek artist is ideal for finessing the gap between the highbrow market and a younger, comic-book fan base. The question remains as to whether art is any the better for the trend. In complying with the exigencies of a marketing drive, is the artist compelled to reduce his work to the status of a trend? The ironic Schiaparelli's humorous prints poked fun at the earnestness of style, and, today, her collections with a surreal twist are still indisputably inventive. Will one be able to say as much of Vuitton-Murakami products?

As if in reaction to a "fast fashion" that flirts with self-sabotage, an opposite tendency hoves into view: "slow fashion" has its sources in ecology and advocates long-lasting clothing. Not only minimalist collector's items by Martin Margiela, but also unique pieces developed by stylist-designers.

The E2 duo, Michèle and Olivier Chatenet, has been working for years recycling and "customizing" luxury clothing, haute couture, and vintage. Theirs are out-of-season one-offs, potpourris from several periods that can readily be compared to artworks. Lastly, there's the sculpture-garment, to be admired rather than worn. In 1966, "12 unwearable dresses in contemporary materials" made of aluminum and cellulose acetate designed by Paco Rabanne were shown on live models to the accompaniment of Pierre Boulez's *Marteau sans Maître*," in a kind of "performance." In its wake, both op (optical) art and abstraction, fully fledged art movements, pursued fashion and design even on to the high street.

In a sign that clothing—if not fashion—is possessed of artistic seriousness, the imagination of certain museum-exhibited artists makes much of the sartorial: recall, for example, Jan Fabre's disconcerting dress made of iridescent beetles, Nicole Tran Ba Vang's frocks and "spray-on" bodysuits decorated with images of what lies under the garment thus "stripping" the body, or that blend the body and its decoration; then there's the gossamer sculptures of Diana Brennan, who recycles, repurposes, and ornaments old clothes. And the poetic, delicate machines of sculptor Jean Tinguely, which, instead of "producing," stimulate the imagination and make mincemeat of convention.

Englishman Alexander McQueen liked to turn his catwalk shows into art happenings: an artistic pose that indulged the uncontrolled gestures of the painter—or, here, the robot!—in the style of Pollock or Twombly.

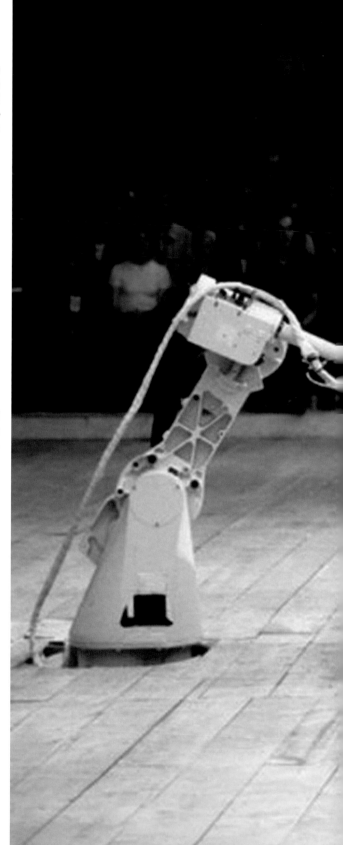

FASHION, STREET, AND ROCK

When agnès b. asks graffiti artists to tag her T-shirts she wants her "clothing to live with the artists who inspired them." Without denying the intellectual, even elitist component of such artistic cachet, agnès b. is also giving back to fashion two facets of its inspiration: the street and music (two fields the designer sponsors via her foundation). Like rock music, the street look has generated many fashion codes identifiable today, adapted by the luxury goods market and even by haute couture, such as slim pants, leather, jeans, studs, baggy jeans, Doc Martens, and the T-shirt, as well as costume jewelry and "rocks" for men.

The influence of the street does not date from yesterday. Born in the 1950s, pop art embraced the icons of industry and consumerism, and soon made inroads into fashion and design: comic books, TV, advertising, everyday objects ironically elevated to the status of inspiration, from Marilyn to Campbell's soup, from Mick Jagger to Mickey Mouse, from American cars to pinups. The goal: to take the gloss off art and, at the same time, to send it careering down the highway to common-or-garden, throwaway, mass-produced consumerism. It was the era of agitators like Andy Warhol, Roy Lichtenstein, Jasper Johns, and Tom Wesselmann. Wesselmann inspired an Yves Saint Laurent collection in 1966: a long dress traversed by a slim female body. Pierre Cardin went for the geometric, op art: short sleeveless dresses with eye-popping designs. The street—a place of protest, youth, and freedom—music, and drug culture composed a social patchwork that fashion made its own: for the first time, people turned their backs on haute couture and invented their own look, in a mix of the hippie, the futuristic, and Carnaby Street. We dressed like Jimi Hendrix or Françoise Hardy and did our hair like Julie Driscoll. More recently, Jeff Koons, Basquiat, and Murakami have bred a new pop art, but their influence on trends is less forceful.

The street has seized power with pop music as its sole competitor. The movies have lost ground to TV, while green concerns are beginning to be felt.

Some designers have boiled down the key ideas from this jumble of influences. Barbara Bui bases a substantial proportion of her brand identity on the language of rock music. Martin Margiela protests in his way against the society of overconsumption, with its logos and media: recycling old clothing, just marking his labels with a number, and refusing to have his photograph taken—even when designing prêt-à-porter for Hermès (from 2000 to 2004).

One marked tendency: rappers, those pure products of the street, of the 'hood, who, joining forces with businessmen, now launch collections of their own.

Joey Starr with Com8, Marc Ecko with Ecko, P. Diddy with Sean John, Wu Tang Clan with Wu Wear, Jay-Z with Rocawear …the list goes on. They are a huge success with customers who may or may not be into hip-hop—the dance style has leeched into theaters, widening its fan base and tribe, and impacting on sports, clubbing, and casual wear generally. In their closets: jeans

in all shapes and sizes—baggy, stonewash, camouflage, fatigues, with elaborate pockets, multiple seams, patterns. Sweatshirts, T-shirts, and jackets are all proudly emblazoned with their logo or the little couture detail that identifies you (pit bull, rhino), and the indispensable baseball cap. Their slogans revel in their bad boy image. For example, the two French creators of P2B have launched T-shirts with the equivalent of "made in the 'burbs, extremely dangerous material" printed on them. Young middle-class guys go for them in a big way. In short, today, any self-respecting rap crew has its own clothing line, or failing that, collaborates with a major label, such as Nike, Reebok, or Puma. Or else he becomes a roving publicist for a relevant brand; Dia Collection, for example, founded by Mohamed Dia (who dresses the NBA).

The world of the night and clubbing has also generated streetwear.

For example Soon and Mokhtar, two DJs, have set up a very popular collection, Bullrot Wear. The inroads made by major brands into this niche are not invariably crowned by success because real streetwear needs a hint of militancy, with attendant codes and in-jokes. **As if to belie their years, some stars sport T-shirts or walk around stamped with logos popular among the "kids," oblivious to the risks of looking like mutton dressed as lamb!**

Luckily, designers are an adaptable bunch: when Madonna or Mylène Farmer orders costumes for gigs from Jean Paul Gaultier or Franck Sorbier, it's in search of that style plus: could anyone forget Gaultier's mortar-shell breastplates for Madonna? As for agnès b., she sweetly confesses that she once sent some leather trousers to David Bowie "after having seen him very poorly turned out [on stage]." The star promptly placed an order.

FASHION AND TECHNOLOGY

Who remembers the "nylon revolution"? The advent of polyester? What about Kevlar, polar fleece, non-iron shirts, stain-resistant carpet, or even stretch leather? The real revolution is in "smart" textiles. It might not be long before we're wearing antipollution garments. Or antivirus, anti-rheumatic, self-heating, or auto-cooling clothes. Jackets that mold to the body or shoes that react to uneven ground; a bra that monitors heart rate; or perhaps luminescent, video, or interactive fabrics.

Élisabeth de Senneville has no doubt about it. A designer with a passion for technology and a tutor at the École Nationale Supérieure des Arts Décoratifs, she has been working on a small, flexible Bluetooth-ready screen that can be incorporated into a windbreaker or T-shirt to transmit and receive messages. With a reputation going back to the 1980s, with prints inspired by pixelization, holograms, and neoprene jackets, she has been concentrating since 2000 on textile research that has more than a hint of sci-fi about it: fiber optics woven into textile materials; antipollution; microencapsulation; photoluminescent textiles and ceramic-impregnated fabrics—in short, the Star Trek wardrobe of the not-so-distant future.

Competitive sports have already resulted in interesting spin-offs: Fastskin, for example, a stretch material finished with fluorinated resin that looks like sharkskin, has made it possible for top-class swimmers in this new Speedo swimsuit to shave off hundredths of a second from their records. An interesting feat of mechanics. But there's more: high-tech fabrics can now be enriched by grafting on molecules or adding conductive polymers. These memorize, resist, protect, and repair; they can self-recycle, and are bioactive. The prototypes are here. For example, by combining

a textile fiber with a steel or copper alloy, shape-memory materials have been manufactured that can remember a physical shape and adapt to it as soon as they encounter body heat. Your shirt closes by itself, the sleeves roll up. Certain labels have branched out into the industrial production of technological jewelry. In a search for more finesse, comfort, and length of life, Ralph Lauren markets a golf jacket made of a revolutionary substance, 3XDRY: ultralight, water-repellent, stain-resistant, it accelerates the evaporation of sweat.

An Anne Valérie Hash jacket that can stand up unaided and records the wearer's movements. It's cut from a material patented by Swiss textile researcher Jakob Schlaepfer.

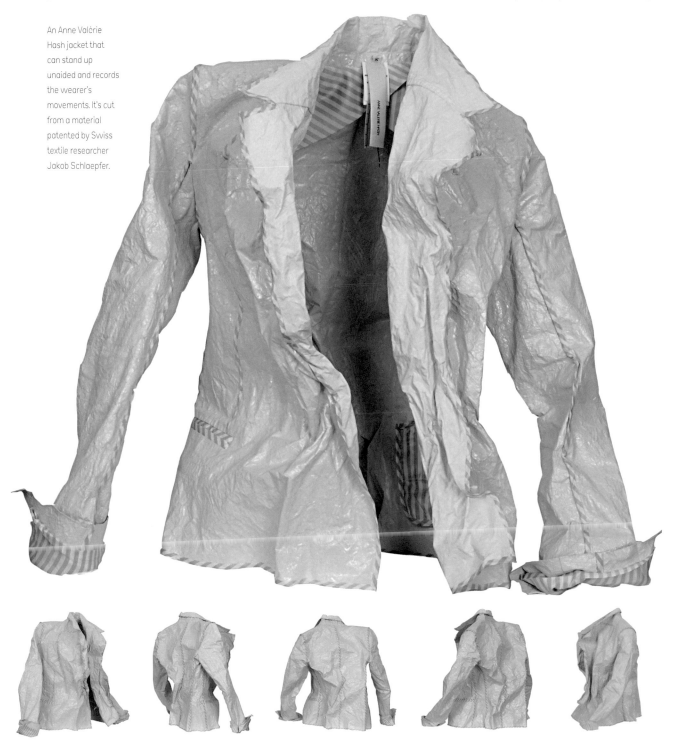

Medicine, surgery, health and safety, space exploration, and the leisure industries are all reaping the rewards of textiles that incorporate active substances before even being spun: anti-bacterial, anti-mold, anti-fungal, anti-mite, anti-UV, odor-eating and, even (for parasols), anti-mosquito. Thanks to nano-encapsulation, designer Adeline André has created scented dresses, Olivier Lapidus a luminescent wedding dress, and Dim and Well pantyhose with cosmetics for the legs.

Genetic engineering has also become involved in the fabrics of tomorrow: after crossing the genes of the silkworm with those of a spider, the resulting silk is five to six times stronger than steel. Lastly, beauty is not entirely absent from these researches: scientists have plumbed the secret of the iridescent shimmer of butterfly wings and bird feathers. New colored fibers are being developed that make use of these novel optical effects.

In short, faced with all these high tech prospects, in the future the utmost chic will surely be to wear a homespun horsehair jacket.

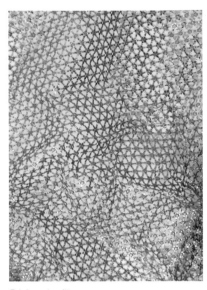

Fabric made with gold thread by Jakob Schlaepfer, detail.

OUT OF THE ORDINARY
A jacket and dress in neoprene and lycra by Élisabeth de Senneville.

RIGHT
AND FACING PAGE
IRIDESCENT
Outfit by Anne Valérie Hash. Close-up: Detail of the bronze thread fabric by Jakob Schlaepfer.

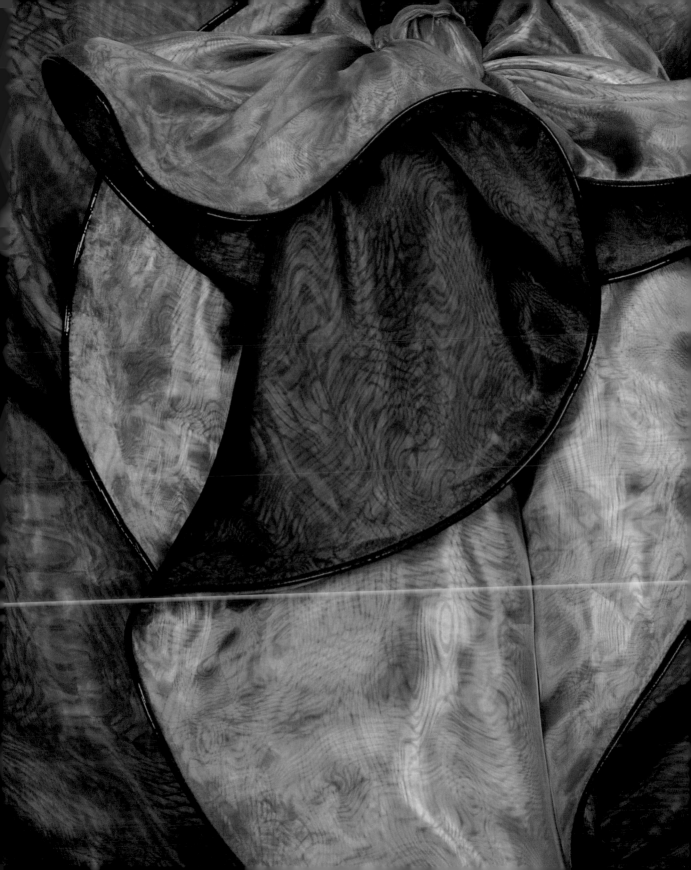

OVERSIZED
SUNGLASSES
And people thought
they'd gone forever
with Jackie O.,
but they're back!
Here, in orange,
by Karl Lagerfeld.

"I HAVE NOTHING TO WEAR!"

The cry that has echoed down the generations. If it provides a convenient excuse for a bout of serious shopping, it doesn't mean that your closet is literally bare. It reflects rather an authentic sense of weariness. So why do we have this feeling? Firstly because, in spite of our "basics," timeless classics, vintage, and other supposed fail-safes that never go out of style, fashion does tire the eyes. Like love, it starts to pale the minute the *coup de foudre* cools down. Depending on the garment, one's passion could be a flash in the pan, or fade into gentle partnership.

Or else, as with all the best couples, it changes and it lasts. If you were unwise enough to invest scads of cash in some harem pants (the ugliest garment ever invented for the female form), disillusionment sets in early because the scales start to fall from your eyes after just five minutes' honest appraisal in the mirror. If, on the other hand, you've managed to unearth pants adapted exactly to your shape, it cuts no ice that fashion exalts bell-bottoms or Lurex slims. You'll keep hold of this basic whose molded buttocks, flat belly, slender thighs, and long legs bring out the best in your physique. All that remains is to adjust the length to the shoe that will thus enjoy the same longevity. For example, Arielle Dombasle, an icon of French fashion, definitively adopted platform soles to which she adjusts every garment—from Notify jeans to a Saint Laurent tuxedo.

There's always *something* to wear. But you have to be able to analyze your walk-in. There are colors, prints, materials, and shapes that do last. You simply have to train your eye to identify the perennial colors, patterns, and cuts. Or learn how to update the fashion of yesteryear into a trend of today.

Examples of basic resources in the event of an "SOS I have nothing to wear!"
Colors: black, midnight blue, camel, "Marlboro" red.
Prints: houndstooth or broken check (careful: the pattern should be a standard size, neither too big nor too small), leopard print (a copy of the real beast: not stylized), lumberjack check, retro polka dots. Stripes are dangerous though: nothing can be more subtly obsolete. Best fallback: the Breton fisherman's top.
Materials: medium-weight jersey, cashmere, merino wool, silk or wool crepe, crisp woolens, cotton poplin.
Shapes: straight rectangle, neither narrow nor figure-hugging, a touch masculine; knee lengths, vintage lines. True vintage (fashion) never goes out of style. For evening, things are both easier and trickier. If you want to play the fashion warrior, it's true you'll often end up with "nothing to wear." Better to cleverly follow the fashions, but give them a personal twist: by unearthing "this season's color" (or garment or accessory) in your closet, or indulging in the impeccable classicism of black, but belted, be-gloved, bedecked *à la mode*.
Another sure thing: exoticism. Since *In the Mood for Love*, we can't imagine anything more feminine than a Chinese dress: long or short, with a print or without, but well-fitting. If you're a bit more daring, the Indian style: long split tunic over trousers narrowing to the leg and corkscrewing down the ankle, in gorgeous colors: a marvel. Avoid going the whole hog though, and leave the jewels and charm bracelets, however twinkly, at home.
Lastly, remind yourself that when our mothers complained, "I have nothing to wear," they meant: "I have nothing to wear for a given circumstance." Today, the acme of chic consists in being mildly out of step with conventional attire. But look out: If you choose a short number for a gala black tie evening because your legs are your strong point, make sure to add sophisticated accessories so you don't feel underdressed.

FACING PAGE
CHALAYAN HUMOR
The English designer of Turkish-Cypriot origin Hussein Chalayan is mad about new high tech fabrics and enjoys ruffling feathers. Here, a vestal virgin at his 2007 show.

"EVERYTHING'S BEEN DONE. THERE'S NOTHING LEFT TO INVENT!"

Of course everything's already been done. And yet fashion doesn't simply go round in circles: it revisits its past, skews it, transforms it. As French chef Joël Robuchon reinvented the mashed potato by adding (humungous quantities of) butter and Jeff Koons rejuvenated pop art with kitsch statues, so in fashion, when John Galliano puts jackets inspired by the Bar suit on the runway for Dior, it is his own personal version: draped, with puff sleeves, swelling back—he explores "the spirit" of the Bar suit, adding his own dash of flamboyance.

Over the years, many designers who have found themselves at the head of a great Parisian fashion house have delved into the archives so as to modernize a label without betraying it. Karl Lagerfeld performed virtuoso marvels with the Chanel suit. As did Alber Elbaz for the Lanvin sheath dress, while Nicolas Ghesquière for Balenciaga kept his distance, being more radical in his widths than the maestro. As for Riccardo Tisci for Givenchy, he decided to turn his back on the classics of the house. He doesn't reinvent, he invents "Tiscis for Givenchy."

Take the trenchcoat, that mainstay of any wardrobe. When designers revisit Columbo's trusty raincoat—or the original "trench" from the trenches—it evolves: into a lamé jacket for evening (Galliano for Dior) or into a sleeveless dress with button-down epaulets (Céline). For Burberry, professionals in such conversions, Christopher Bailey puts the zipper in the front, adds material round sleeves or base, makes it bristle with leather, or reimagines it in suede (thus rendering it utterly useless in a downpour). Jean Paul Gaultier preserves the original, but brazens it out with a belt flush to the skin. Nathalie Rykiel for Sonia Rykiel makes a dual reference—in transparent vinyl it casts a sideways glance at 1960s op art.

To reinvent itself, style can also heed the call of technology. A new material may spawn hybrid fashions. For example, elastic and washable leather jeans by Jitrois are different from denim jeans and distinct again from leather pants. Knitted fur is neither fur nor knitwear. Novel resins and 3-D sketches permit unheard-of liberties: sculpture shoes (Prada), shoes with back-to-front heels (Marc Jacobs), and mutant pumps-cum-clogs (Alexander McQueen). Tomorrow's fibers (see the chapter "Fashion and Technology") will provide a new feel, a new fall, a new rigidity, engendering yet still more new lines.

Over time, what can be worn has changed in line with what is thought of as decent, or indecent. Ever since Saint Laurent elevated black chiffon into a classic of sexy elegance, fashion has been constantly reinterpreting the idea of transparency. The result: lingerie and underclothing now form integral parts of an outfit: the Calvin Klein boxer waistband or the thong above the belt on a pair of jeans, or the Chantal Thomass bra peeking out of a Zadig et Voltaire sweater.

Fashion is a language. If one knows its vocabulary, one still has to master its grammar, the rules that change. Subtly.

FASHION MYTHS

FASHION CAN BURN YOU OUT!

Our wardrobes tell more about us than just our style choices. They betray our likings—but also our weaknesses and our neuroses.
Why do some women buy skintight dresses they never go out in? Why do others fall for bright colors but are always seen in black? Why do some "clean out" their closets, and others not? And why do so many men—in Paris at least—take refuge in the new modern uniform, black T-shirt with black pants and jacket? Why do some prefer good old corduroy when others always wear their jeans too short over ankle socks? As with how we walk, eat, drive a car, fashion is revealing. As philosopher Thomas Carlyle observed in 1834 in *Sartor Resartus*: "Neither in tailoring nor in legislating does man proceed by mere Accident, but the hand is ever guided on by mysterious operations of the mind. In all his Modes, and habilatory endeavours, an Architectural Idea will be found lurking; his Body and the Cloth are the site and materials whereon and whereby his beautified edifice, of a Person, is to be built…. if the Cut betoken Intellect and Talent, so does the Color betoken Temper and Heart."

We should become more conscious of these "habilatory endeavors" and learn how to make them serve us. Because in urban environments, our sartorial image, like our body language, can either smooth understanding or be misconstrued. The psychological interpretations of a sunken chest, of a shoulder higher than the other, of leaning the head to one side, or habitual gestures (such as crossing the arms, pulling the earlobe, rubbing the nose or thigh, or even waddling with one's feet turned inward) are well documented. In addition to such gestural clues, the attitudes our apparel presents to the world—and to ourselves—offer pointers to our foibles, blind spots, and self-image. At ease? Uptight? Indecisive? Hung up? Without having to indulge in retail Gestalt therapy, it may not be uninteresting to correct—or to consciously adopt—certain ways of behaving in order to improve our daily lives, to enrich our knowledge of ourselves.

We should be lucid about our impulse buys, about our gaffes in the mall, about our incapacity to off-load "old friends." We should be able to accept them or change them. **In short, to transform our knowledge of the rag trade into an analytical tool, even into a weapon of conquest, of others and of ourselves.**

"STRIPES? WITH CHECKS? HOW AWFUL!"

In the days of Vivienne Westwood, Paul Smith, and Dries Van Noten, this kind of exclamation signals lamentable ignorance. All and sundry now possess consummate skill in mixing and matching prints, playing with dissonance, flirting with the "bad taste" much in evidence in certain manor houses in the outskirts of Edinburgh. The English kicked things off, "deconstructing" clan tartan, overlapping lines, swapping colors. As a punk pioneer, Westwood built them into insane constructions, cajoling what had been a cloth of eminently manly connotations into bustiers, long-line bras, or poufs for a crazy countess. Her compatriot Paul Smith also specializes in sending serious menswear into a spin, with natty floral prints on the wristbands and collars of his striped men's shirts. Meanwhile Dries Van Noten combines distorted checks or ethnic patterns with gaudy stripes, leopard prints with impressionism, great gilded blooms that almost put the teeth on edge.

Juggling prints and patterns is a risky business. One needs to educate the eye. Once it is trained though, the results can totally rejuvenate a look. The first to mix and match prints was Emmanuel Ungaro in the 1970s. An admirer of women clad in veils and chiffon, in waisted and draped lines, with the help of Sonja Knapp, he created his own fabrics. On his muse, the actress Anouk Aimée, he combined stripes and checks and dots in subtle graphic interplay. Ungaro however kept to related tones, his colors did not "clash." Yves Saint Laurent, perhaps under the influence of exoticism, essayed a more daring palette: red and violet, orange and fuchsia, or green and blue. "Heresies" that he transcended, inventing an allure that verges on provocation. Influencing our tastes, he transformed the "done thing."

Lastly, let us not forget the *sapeurs* of the Congo, African men with a dandy eye for mix and match: lacking money but with a wild imagination fueled by an African approach to style, they have imposed garish colors, high contrasts, and lunatic shoes on the street, without shedding the trad suit and spotless Borsalino. A high-wire act, at once incredibly kitsch and life-enhancing.

Still, if one's a little unsure of oneself, it's hard to wear a polka-dot shirt over striped pants. Keep to something plainer and, for that fashion touch, fall back on a saturated monochrome with an accessory in a contrasting shade: Mediterranean blue-green or turquoise, with jewels (or shoes) in apple green. Or blue-purple/violet/hot pink with a red belt. With a dark complexion, one can go for mustard-saffron-ocher with an airforce-blue beret.

FACING PAGE
MAD BAG LADY
Vivienne Westwood puts tartan through its paces. Here, the Sun King makes an entrance, but hybridized with rock anti-conformism.

"HAND KNITS ARE OVER!"

In fashion everything goes out of style, and nothing is ever dead. It's the only domain where nothing really disappears, everything can be "reborn," reinterpreted. An inexhaustible goldmine, nostalgia is a constant inspiration to designers.
Laura Ashley florals of the 1960s? Hippie kaftans of the 1970s? 1980s leg-of-mutton sleeves? Not to mention crochet vests, square-toed shoes, nylon and rayon, granny prints, and garish colors. These horrors which one once thought would only feature in documentary films return in force to become the dernier cri.

Miuccia Prada, a champion at this game, has even managed to put the nondescript secretary look back on the agenda—dull checks, prints like old curtains, high-buttoned neck, chunky heels—but instead of sending us to sleep, the outfit, thanks to its details, is reenergized with chic. Her compatriots Dolce 8 Gabbana, meanwhile, tap into the codes of the Sicilian widow that used to so terrify Italian girls—black mid-calf dress and black lace—but add plunging necklines and see-through fabrics to reveal a touch of come-hither lingerie.

Apart from the natural osmosis by which one generation takes up elements from its predecessor, it's the designer know-how that's key. Bell-bottoms are no longer cut from the same denim; crochet tunics are more neatly produced than in the past; updated miniskirts are straight or tulip shaped, not trapezoid; grandma's print patterns are disposed differently and on new materials; leg-of-mutton sleeves do not have quite the same proportions; strong colors are distributed in small doses, or meld into a more ethnic look.

Even retro brands that rely on the principle of nostalgia reconfigure their classics. For example, Emilio Pucci's emblematic 1960s silk jerseys and acid psychedelic arabesques prints may conjure up those go-getting, devil-may-care, free-and-easy times, but they don't actually reproduce the designs. Much appreciated by the jetset, the style was worn on evening gowns at fashionable evening parties, on trapezoid tunics over slacks, and on skiwear before falling out of favor after twenty years or so. Revived by Pucci's daughter, Laudomia, and then bought out by LVMH in 2000, the house was once again the nec plus ultra of style thanks to Christian Lacroix, recruited for a few seasons back in 2003. Today in vintage boutiques Pucci pieces where the design follows the cut are fought over. In 1960s France, Daniel Tribouillard, alias Leonard, beguiled our mothers and grandmothers with similar qualities, before falling on hard times—**perhaps it, too, might benefit from a revival spearheaded by someone whose talent for marketing matches Leonard's genuine skill with patterns.**

GRACE KELLY
The deathless
Hermès bag,
designed in the
1930s by Robert
Dumas (great-
grandson of founder
Thierry Hermès).
It was adopted
in 1958 by the
princess of Monaco,
Grace Kelly, who
collected many
different sizes
and colors.

LESSONS IN VINTAGE FASHION

WHAT IS IT?

The word "vintage" is normally employed in the English-speaking world to mean a fine wine of a particularly good year. In the world of style, thanks to lovers of retro, vintage fashion is more than just a fashion: it's become a culture. An addiction. Even an intoxication. A fine 1950s sheath dress can make the head spin as fast as any Bordeaux grand cru. As fashion gains more and more in importance in our daily lives, in our budgets, and in our museums, its history now forms part of our collective consciousness. Any reasonably urbane person has heard of Dior's New Look, of Cardin's trapeze line; we may be able to recognize a Courrèges logo, and many can identify a Saint Laurent Mondrian dress. These signs are now integral to the style-conscious landscape. Sometimes they are commercially exploited by major popular brands. Style bureaus, vast studios of industrial design, have long noted this evolution, an increased awareness that has become almost universal.

Going, going, gone!

Sotheby's, Christie's, Philips, Artcurial, and others hold sales of vintage fashion: some even have a special department and they are regularly entrusted with jewels, bags, and garments, signed and/or dated. A sale of Hermès bags at Christie's is an unmissable event that risks degenerating into a fashionista free-for-all. As for period furniture, prices can climb exponentially. The mythical Kelly that is sold for approximately 7,500 dollars in stores today can rise to more than three times that if it's a sapphire-blue croc made in 1998. Vintage fashion has its collectors, its price tags, and even its investors. But true amateurs rarely sell on. They just can't.

COLLECTOR'S ITEM
Ensemble designed by Gabrielle Chanel around 1930 and sold in Paris in February 2010 by auctioneers Cornette de Saint Cyr. Pure Chanel refinement: the coat's silk lining matches the fabric on the dress.

What people like about the vintage style

Vintage clothing reeks of nostalgia, of originality, of reminiscences of past times. Ah, those stiff woolen jackets from the 1940s and 1950s! With less twist, the yarn has a dryness, a mildly blocked feel that imposes a sense of presence. Horsehair padded shoulderpads provided width more delicately than the foam ones of today. And the sheer number of stitches and ribs, of buttons and details (sometimes a little too many) shows the length of time spent on its execution, a taste for abundance. Vintage clothing does not smack of time-and-motion or rationalized mass production. Lastly, nothing is more endearing than one of those large retro labels hand-sewn onto a wonderfully thick satin coat lining: often written in elaborate script, they are not in fact mere logos, but sonorous, out-of-date surnames, while the French ones are inscribed *Fabriqué en France,*" instead of the conventional oxymoron of "Made in France."

VINTAGE ICON
Before becoming
princess of Monaco,
Grace Kelly placed
her natural grace
in the service of
American fashion
as much as of the
cinema. Here she
is ultramodern
in capri pants given
a feminine touch by
a gathered half-skirt
and mules with
platform soles,
leaning over a
designer armchair
virtually identical
to her straw hat.

Why vintage?

Because the piece will be unique and rich in meaning. In a globalized world, amid the stylistic homogeneity imposed by industrial clothing, vintage fashion represents one last (accessible) island of personalization. Are you weary of brands with worldwide reach that one sees in the same store windows everywhere, from Armani to Zara via Prada and H&M? Then vintage is for you. You just have to look for it. Whether you're a well-heeled lady, a penniless student, a man who appreciates fine fabrics, or simply seeking something special in the fashion jungle, vintage brings that touch of soul lacking in standardized apparel. Moreover, certain stars—Angelina Jolie, Natalie Portman, not to mention a host of French actresses—sometimes forsake their designers for an historic article they are sure never to see on a rival. Moreover, once you've learned how to recognize authenticity, a vintage piece is in general well worth the price and—more crucially—never goes out of style. Better still: with a bit of luck, it'll become a collector's item. Your pride and joy.

HOW TO IDENTIFY A STYLE

Zippers can provide a pointer to precisely dating a piece: they were made of metal until the 1930s; placed on seams to the side until the 1950s; and then mid-back for dresses and skirts. Quality needle-work (sewing of the zipper, hems, biascut) often indicates vintage couture. Moreover, it should also be recalled that clothing from before World War II did not yet flaunt "designer labels." Lastly, take care of venerable but fragile garments that may not stand up to the daily grind. And remain lucid as to styling: the 1980s with their leg-of-mutton sleeves and oversize shoulders were never hugely becoming, it cannot be denied. Our preferred years? From 1920 to 1960, the best in terms of style, those which saw the birth and growth of both haute couture and prêt-à-porter. With their ageless patina, the 1950s, inspired by the great Hollywood movies, are in general the most flattering (and the most expensive).

UNIQUE PIECE
FOR A STAR
In 2009, to avoid
bumping into a
fellow thespian
wearing the same
model, Penélope
Cruz chose a
vintage dress by
Balmain, from the
period when the
collections were
designed by Oscar
de la Renta.

SO STYLISH!
Irresistible tweed
suit by Pierre Cardin
(1953). Aged thirty-
one, the young
designer had just
founded his house,
after beginning in the
women's suits and
coats department
at Christian Dior.
His skill shines
through in this
ensemble that
one would still
be delighted to
be seen in today.

the 1920s

The birth of the era of assembly-line production influenced fashion and the arts, leading them to enter into a fertile dialogue. In the shadow of Picasso and Braque and of the dressmakers Madeleine Vionnet, Jeanne Lanvin, Jean Patou, and Lucien Lelong, the lines became less fussy, stripped back to essentials: cut, construction, fabric. To eyes captivated by cubism and futurism ornaments suddenly looked out-of-date or overloaded, and were promptly banished. Sexy new lines emerged that bared more flesh; cabaret took to the stage, America and jazz were top of the bill, while, in the grip of the Roaring Twenties, Gay Paris tripped the light fantastic.

SCULPTURAL

This sheath dress by Madeleine Vionnet shows her genius in drapery and biascut. She brought out the best in women's curves, eliminated the corset, but also invented a recognizable brand and was the first to show concern for the welfare of her workers, making sure they took vacations.

MODERN GEOMETRY

Made by the Soeurs Callot in 1924, this outfit offers a digest of many of the characteristics of those years: sobriety (in hairstyle and jewelry), clear lines, a tubular structure (biascut asymmetrical tunic over a wraparound skirt), simplicity (purity of silk, just two tones; the train; the string of pearls). Marvelously flattering for the body.

the 1930s

The crash of 1929 ruined many a millionaire, but the frenzy of the Roaring Twenties and its lavish soirées jived on unabated. The names of Hollywood stars were on everyone's lips. Marlene Dietrich, Greta Garbo, Mae West, Jean Harlow, and Joan Crawford didn't just wear clothes by American costumers, they also "sold" the best of Paris couture on the big screen: Vionnet, Lanvin, and Schiaparelli. Slinky-lined sheath dresses for evening trimmed and refined the figure, day dresses were worn close to the body with little box pleats and art deco designs. Rayon poured onto the market, women started to sunbathe and play sports, and "beach pyjamas" made their appearance. Even today, in furniture as in fashion, the 1930s remain a highwater mark.

the 1940s

The war brought rations, people scrimped and saved and "made do." The consequence was the appearance of suits with severe lines in long-lasting fabrics. Panache was not de rigueur. Lines were simplified: collars narrower, lapels fewer, and decorations restricted to clever little details of buttoning and topstitch. Fabrics? Synthetic, recycled woolens, felt, taffeta, corduroy. Women did their bit in pants and trenchcoats. Occupied France no longer held supremacy and the Americans entered the fray: Claire McCardell, Adolph Schuman, Adrian. Their sober, flattering, easy-to-wear lines marked the onset of the casual. Evening wear was not neglected though, as seen in sumptuous sheath dresses.

UNADULTERATED FEMININITY
The New Look spirit took to the town in numerous guises. Here, in Berlin in 1957: crisp ottoman (with perhaps a tulle underskirt) affords an ampleness that contrasts with the slender bodice, underscored by a wide belt. Simple scoop neck, no added decoration.

SOBRIETY
A typical outfit from the war era, by Jacques Fath (1944): mildly flared skirt with broad straps and shortened due to the shortage of fabric; although there are no frills and flounces a hint of luxury transpires in the ample sleeves on the blouse. The shoulders are padded, the figure astutely elevated on platform shoes.

the 1950s

Industry went into overdrive. Dior launched his New Look, the fashion(able) expression of this newfound prosperity: he widened the skirt, made the tulle underskirt a must, lowered hemlines. He narrowed waists and bust, enlarged the peplum. In the eyes of some editorialists, such collections were no longer adapted to modern life. Cristóbal Balenciaga, on the other hand, loosened the cut. His noticeably less waisted jackets with softer shoulders freed up movement. Coats billowed, collars vanished. The first Chanel suit in braid-trimmed tweed appeared in 1954: aged 71, Chanel had returned to the fray. But her young customers, in pants and slacks, made their own demands. Givenchy launched his "sack dress." Cardin unveiled his "bubble dress." In short, the generation gap was opening up.

the 1960s

Swinging, joyous, and mad about color, the 1960s metamorphosed the image of woman. Illustrated by Twiggy, the tendency oscillated between androgyny and Lolita. Knees came into view, then (thin) thighs beneath a miniskirt or a sleeveless A-line dress over which was thrown a maxi-coat that almost brushed the ankle. There were forays into knitwear catsuits by Courrèges, Ferragamo flats with rectangular buckles, silver vinyl thighboots or square-toed boots, and no one would dream of leaving the house without their pea-coat or shiny op art raincoat.

UNDER FULL SAIL
Even Cardin, totally committed to clean lines, could not remain immune to the diaphanous loose-fitting curves of the times. In 1978, he designed loose-fitting tunics, but still paid great attention to the construction.

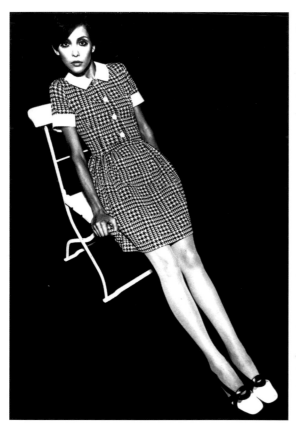

SWEET AND INNOCENT?
Child-woman sporting a natty shirtwaist dress with goodie-two-shoes collar in 1969, smoothed down, childlike hairstyle, at odds with the full-on makeup and huge eyes. At the end of her long legs (thinner than they would have been ten years previously), the flat shoes match the black-and-white patterned dress.

the 1970s

Hippie follies predominated in resolutely cool young styles that were impregnated with folklore from remote lands, with India at the head. Flowers were all the rage—Cacharel's Liberty—dresses and tunics in layers of silk or cotton, DIY (macramé bags and vests, tie-dye), fuzzy lines, prints mixed and broad-brush, psychedelic flowers, checks, art-studio swathes of color. This was the advent of a generation of young Anglo-Saxon designers buoyed up by a punk-ethno-disco hotchpotch: Ossie Clark, Oscar de la Renta, Geoffrey Beene, Bill Blass, Ralph Lauren, Diane Von Furstenberg, and, of course, the Westwood-McLaren tandem and their London boutique, Seditionaries.

the 1980s

This is the decade of "power dressers" with quarterback shoulder-pads, frightening leg-of-mutton sleeves, and wasp waists, sheathed in armor-plated suits signed by Mugler, Montana, and Alaïa. Thanks to Jean Paul Gaultier, transgender humor and a shot of punk short-circuited the pushiness. Elsewhere, Japanese creators Rei Kawakubo (Comme des Garçons) and Yohji Yamamoto took the opposite course: hewn from the rough, asymmetrical, not very sexy, but subtly put-together. Kenzo triumphed with a cheery blend of folklore: flowery Russian fabrics, Chinese collars, Indian silks and woolens, while Miyake worked his charm with shimmering pleats.

MILD PROTEST

Ann Demeulemeester's archetypal silhouette dates to 1994. Over the years, she has constantly refashioned and refined its stylishness: sober colors and handmade fabrics, asymmetry and overlay—her pieces are made to last, in keeping with the 1990s that rebelled against waste and fickleness.

AUTHORITY

Thierry Mugler's women are sometimes warriors, sometimes vamps. Pushing the suit to a paroxysm of sexuality, he turns women into curvy-hipped, cinch-waisted dominatrixes or soldiers. His dresses and jackets, with their unexpected openings and stitching, capture the morphology to perfection.

the 1990s

After the frenzy of the 1980s, fashion began to downsize to lower consumption, to recycling, miserabilism even. There's grunge (Kurt Cobain of *Nirvana*) and his terrible logger's shirt, and the advent of "basics": jeans, trainers, T-shirt, K-way. Sports brands launch fully fledged collections, jogging pants are seen in town, while daring hybrids become classics: suits with Converses and T-shirt. Already there were whiffs of "vintage": the 1970s with platform soles and 1950s-style bustiers of the *Spice Girls*. Catwalks reeled to the creative zest of the Belgians: Martin Margiela, Ann Demeulemeester, Dries Van Noten, and Dirk Bikkembergs—their trends: minimalism, arty, social comment.

HOW TO BUY AND WEAR VINTAGE FASHION

A vintage piece in conjunction with a contemporary outfit immediately makes you stand out. It shows perceptiveness and a refusal to bend the knee to the decrees of fashion. If you're petite and slim, clothes from the 1920s and 1930s will suit you perfectly, as long as you avoid oversize graphics. If you have curves and a bust but a slender waist, the 1950s are tailor-made for you. Long legs and a boyish figure? Then it's the 1960s. If you like dressing up then go the whole hog: dress, jewelry, bags, shoes, and even a hairstyle make a more humorous statement than the full Chanel. If not, a fitted 1950s or boxy 1960s jacket more than hold their own with today's jeans, trousers, or a skirt. And nothing is more enduring than a wonderfully feminine belted Bardot dress, and nothing more elegant than Clark Gable or Rock Hudson pants (with a crease). To escape the tyranny of the It bag (an exorbitantly priced designer accessory suddenly declared a must-have), carry a true retro bag to offset that modern look. And if you can't afford jewelry, imposing vintage costume ornaments will give a lift to any outfit for a fraction of the cost of the real thing.

Of course, if you have the wherewithal, you should go to Didier Ludot, an Aladdin's cave of vintage haute couture beneath the arcades of Palais Royal in Paris. People visit this boutique as they would a clothing museum, emerging from it enriched with knowledge, culture, and beauty.

WHAT YOU MUST HAVE (LADIES)

Vintage fashion is all very well, but how do you do it without looking as if you're off to a costume ball? The secret is to train your eye to identify the truly timeless lines, the finest fabrics, the best finishes and details that combine to make a unique piece, a classic that will outlast the seasons. In general, a well-chosen garment lasts a lifetime as, without inevitably appearing vintage, it goes with everything. It might be a peacoat, a twinset, a straight skirt in a quality fabric, a little black dress, pin-striped trousers, a bag, a men's jacket, or a pair of pumps.

**Buy tomorrovv's
vintage today.**

FACING PAGE
One can play
with classic forms,
pepping them up with
unexpected colors:
turquoise peacoat
and bronze low-
heeled shoes.
The white shirt
remains unbeatable;
here by Rei Kawakubo
Comme des Garçons
for H&M, with a
narrow, preeminently
Japanese collar.
The strongest
piece—already a
vintage classic—is the
1950s coat without
buttons, in red raw
silk that livens up
any outfit. But it could
just as well be an
embroidered coat,
Chinese or Indian.
Never forget jewelry
to top off, turn on, or
jazz up. A good bag
and pumps can stay
the course over
several seasons.

RIGHT
Popularized by
the 1950s and
2000s, leopard print
is never out of style,
especially on a well-
cut trench coat.

WHAT YOU MUST HAVE (GENTLEMEN)

Your choice is somewhat easier because the range is narrower. But to make the most of your wardrobe and yet retain a suggestion of originality, you, too, need to be able to recognize an impeccable cut, classy materials, and standout detailing. For example, a trench coat, neither too broad nor overburdened with straps and pockets, an Aran sweater in good wool or cashmere will make you look good, a pair of real shoes (not sneakers), and a suit that keeps its shape, neither tight nor baggy. One basic rule: the seam should precisely follow the line of your shoulders.

Select your ultimate classic now!

LEFT
Accessories—those telltales—remain crucial: cufflinks for grander evenings (avoid novelty numbers), belts (the buckle should not be too shiny), oxfords, scarves (English college types or wider couture models), watch. A good vest with a well-cut shirt (without a contrasting colored collar) goes over jeans as well as Cary Grant pants with a crease.

FACING PAGE
A Prince of Wales check flannel suit outlasts the seasons. Note the details: pressed pleated pants, real buttonholes on the cuffs, panel pockets on the jacket, and the lapel, neither

too wide nor too
narrow. It is a good
basic that can either
be loosened up
with sweater
or colored shirt,
or played straight
with a tie.

THE VINTAGE DRESS FOR WOMEN

A dress represents the perfect terrain for recognizing style trends down the ages. In those distant times, one wouldn't have been satisfied with a single pretty going-out dress. According to the occasion, it would have been out of the question to wear an "afternoon" number for an exhibition opening at eight. Designer, or inspired by a couturier, your dress and jewelry were a social telltale. Today, according to your vital statistics, your tastes, and the circumstances, vintage offers just the right piece, and gives the nod to history too: whether for a morning appointment, theater date, dinner party, gallery opening, or wedding, vintage is infinitely adaptable. And, as it is

1940

1950

1950

DANCE ON MADISON AVENUE
In emerald-green taffeta, mid-length, it has a touch of the Lana Turners. Room to maneuver is provided by a biascut panel beneath the bust and by the crisp, snappy fabric that falls well. The fall is underlined by the pleated sash in eau de nile that floats to either side at the back. It should be in silk chiffon for an airier look, but due to the restrictions it's synthetic.

COCKTAIL PARTY AT PEGGY'S
This might be a day dress, but closer observation reveals singular refinement. Exceptional haute couture quality silk forms a gorgeous ground for a sumptuous rose print. Above the waist, two decorative folds cross beneath the bust. The armholes whose bias-cut edges are in the same fabric as the dress encroach slightly on the top of the shoulder for that dressier look. The folds from the waist are flat and broad to avoid the dress billowing. The hem at the back is longer than at the front, imposing a posture of rounded shoulders and projecting hips typical of 1950s models. Finally, the skirt is lined in tulle for width and fall. It can be accessorized with a belt.

A LITTLE CHAT
A summer outfit in silk twill. This skirt too has broad flat pleating to forestall puffiness. Triple topstitch folds start out at the waist to form a star at the bust. The waist is high, providing length for the figure. The short jacket with its tailored collar and three-quarter sleeves is lined in taffeta. It can be thrown over the shoulders or carried as an accessory. Fluid and light, the whole outfit moves well.

no longer beyond the pale to essay "afternoon wear" in the evening, you'll always be smarter and more original than someone sporting hundreds of dollars of denim. You can be yourself in vintage—as well as sure you'll never see the same dress on another. If, like the majority of us, you have to put the brakes on your clothing expenditure, explore the markets. From London and New York to Los Angeles, from Denver and Chicago to Amsterdam, Brussels, or Tokyo, there's hardly a city that does not have its vintage and retro shops, jumble sales, or natty boutiques— no stone should be left unturned.

1960 **1970** **1980**

PSYCHEDELIC FIESTA

Superb 1960s print with stylized plants looking as if it been painted in gouache, set off by a simple trapeze cut. The fabric? Nylon voile over an orange crepe lining. The three-quarter sleeves flare slightly, while the back is no less intriguing: with a square neckline, to add fluidity it incorporates two pleated panels.

FOLLOW MY LEADER

Another version of the eternal little black dress. Here, with a hint at a shirt (the buttoning is just for show) in wool crepe and cotton voile hand-painted with dotted lines forming little circles. To give fall, the outfit is lined in a weighty taffeta; save for the sleeves, see-through and secured by a shirt cuff with covered buttons. It can be brightened up with a vividly colored scarf, loosely tied, or a thin belt.

FACE POWDER

Soft pink wool crepe on a suit baptized Le Dix, by Balenciaga; like his perfume and like the address of his house, which opened in 1948 at number 10, avenue George V in Paris. This ensemble, with bulky shoulders that make it look quintessentially 1980s, in fact probably dates to 1968, the year Balenciaga retired. He was a maestro of construction, with a cut that endowed his designs with enigmatic volumes. The tulip skirt displays a pair of gathers to the side. The shoulder and armholes form a single piece, sewn on by a flap to the bust. A true feat of dressmaking. The back of the jacket is lightly gathered from the waist, the whole lined entirely in silk, in the same pink, including the pockets, with the luxurious detailing and the same gathers to the back of the jacket as outside. The two parts of the suit can also be worn separately for a less showy effect.

THE VINTAGE WARDROBE FOR MEN

Of course, there is the eternal black or pinstripe double-breasted suit in crisp wool—marginally banker, slightly Al Capone: a collector's item adored by fans of vintage who give it a twist with two-tone shoes. But there's much more besides: blazers, safari jackets, blousons, check pants, high-waisted trousers with creases, retro wraps, and vests. Watch old movies to learn how to recognize clothing from a particular era. Stiffer fabrics, horsehair shoulder padding, buckram to prevent the jacket losing its shape. And tidy details in the buttons and linings, and visible stitching.

WHERE COULD I HAVE PUT THE YACHT?
Often thought of as eccentric, checks can also be perennially stylish. Made here by the English house Aquascutum, they are cut in a manner that will flatter any leg length. Worn with a Cerruti 1881 blazer from the 1970s, it composes an impeccable outfit that exudes the man of taste, but with a hint of fantasy.

ON THE GALLOPS
Attractive beige-caramel tones: with tweed jodhpurs by Banana Republic, the light woolen jacket with a Mao collar and buttoned placket for that couture look dates from the 1980s (Et Vous). Of good length, it stops at the buttocks so as not to compress the figure. Worn with a Sonia Rykiel sweater of a mossy hue, one half expects to see riding boots and a stableman!

CORDUROY FOREVER
With its geography teacher connotations, corduroy has long been denigrated, but now its broader incarnation has become genuinely "intellectual," while narrower (here unearthed in red ocher at Victoire in the 1990s), it is quite simply "fashion." Naturally it should be combined with an unexpected color, like this purple shirt in fine-wale corduroy unearthed at the supermarket Monoprix.

SHOOTING PARTY

The Austrians do not only make Sachertorte. They also invented a hunting jacket in rugged wool; warm and hardly altered since 1960, it will not crease. To give it a more urban twist, add a designer scarf emblazoned with a delicate print (Paul Smith), updating it with a pair of pale army pants.

ZERMATT IN SUMMER

Boiled wool: another fabric that keeps its style and scores highly for comfort and warmth. By Cacharel, this jacket is unlined, with stitched edging and pockets for elegance. Bright red, it can brighten the grayest complexion. Mountaineer's knickerbockers with leather ties offer a welcome change for muscular calves without appearing stringy. Lastly, for that urban touch, a pretty silk 1940s scarf with a geometrical pattern in the same tones.

HIGHLAND FLING

Yet more pants with checks at once appealingly cut and original: in Old England wool, high-waisted with two pleats to each side and cuffs, it is here worn with a spencer jacket and a 1950s evening vest. With light fawn derbies, this ensemble unites England, Wales, and Scotland with a bang!

MAFIOSO?
Decidedly massive,
if the oversize
fringes of these
Prada loafers verge
on bad taste, they
flaunt the luxury
of glossy leather.

For centuries men exercised their imagination in competing with each other to attract. In the Middle Ages, for example they exhibited their legs and thighs more insolently than a teenage girl in a miniskirt.

These "leggings" were called hose; red, blue, or black, they hung at the waist from aglets or cords. Above, these men wore a pourpoint or doublet, a short padded jacket—the ancestor of the bulletproof vest in that it afforded additional protection beneath armor.

In the 1660s at the court of the young Louis XIV, who inaugurated the two-century hegemony of "French taste" over every court in Europe, the wardrobe of both sexes was like a firework display. Women boasted underskirts, sumptuous pleats, precious stones, pearls, and brocade. But, at their sides, the men showed no less panache, strapped into colorful, long, fitted jackets boasting a cloud of lace, their legs sheathed in stockings. Examining paintings of the time, one is astounded by the shimmer of fabrics and a kind of feminine, precious grace among these gentlemen, further enhanced by their wigs.

From the nineteenth century, luxury was conveyed by greater sobriety. To advertise one's wealth became vulgar. Thus the path was paved for dandyism, an obsession with understated elegance pursued to the last detail. Dandyism, embodied by the Englishman George Bryan Brummell, who treated it as a profession, uncoupled good taste from its association with social position: in spite of his origins—or because of them—Brummell, the son of a private secretary, lavished care on every component of his attire to create an ideal image of the man of distinction.

Smart without ostentation, though he declared that "if people turn around to look at you in the street, you are not well-dressed," dandyism did not exclude a dash of eccentricity. Aloof, insolent, ironic, Brummell attracted disciples among the nobility and aristocracy solely through the gracefulness of his statements (both verbal and sartorial): the Prince of Wales, Lord Byron, Barbey d'Aurevilly, Oscar Wilde, all celebrated his art of sophisticated living in their life and/or writings. Alas, he ended up ruined by gambling, prison, lunacy, and paralysis.

One can adopt his precepts today almost without alteration. His first rule was that clothes should not be too fitted as this made the body ugly and often ridiculous. The second dealt with the proportions between top and bottom, one's figure appearing lighter in clothes that taper from top to bottom. Though today it is harder to keep track of the sartorial codes, this geometric rule still holds good.

Circumnavigating the hippie phenomenon—whose exoticism was merely a pretext for letting-it-all-hang-out—we come to the uniformization of the industrial era, when only the new visibility of the homosexual community ushered in a return to stylishness among males. And it was a soccer player, David Beckham, who, in the early 2000s, gave the green light to heterosexuals to once again cultivate a desire to please, developing a sociotype: the "metrosexual" (an expression coined in 1994 by a London journalist, Mark Simpson, to describe the emergence of a prosperous urban male whose own person becomes a "love object").

According to studies by advertising guru Marian Salzman, in ten years' time this "right to narcissism" will go hand in hand with the "abandonment of traditional male aspirations such as wealth and power," redirecting the emphasis onto emotional values. Perhaps. More circumspect, in *Masculins singuliers* (Robert Laffont) Swiss journalist Paul Ackermann describes "an evolved man, who is no longer encumbered by male chauvinist cultural baggage." That, too, is as may be.

MENSWEAR

FACING PAGE

SEQUINS AND
ROMANTICISM
Anne Valérie
Hash deconstructs
the military jacket.

LEFT
RAW RECRUIT
At Lanvin, Alber
Elbaz goes in for
hand-weave and
camouflage.

Macho or not, these men see clothing as a socio-aesthetic experience. Since to destabilize the rigid conventions of the male uniform and reinvent the dandy—even for an eighteenth-century gentleman—requires tact as well as audacity.

Male style, like women's style, has gained in complexity, in diversity. In the beginning, it was details that made the man: vibrant linings (such as those by Ozwald Boateng who was the first to introduce color into Savile Row suits), prints on the cuffs of a Paul Smith shirt, or the inverted lapels by Thierry Mugler. Jean Paul Gaultier's man-skirt in 1985, though smacked of a "happening" rather than everyday wear, just as Versace's glitziness remained the preserve of showbiz. Those fond of something more fluid initially headed to Armani, who dared to remove lining and padding from jackets, enshrining the legendary relaxed look of Italian chic. In those years, one had to go on a pilgrimage to Milan if one wanted to assuage a natural desire for variety without breaking the bank.

Since 2000 creators, followed more timidly by mass-market retailers, have started to change, shadowing social trends. Between androgyny and irony, men initially widened their palette beyond the sempiternal beige-black-brown-navy, plus check and stripes. Take a bow Dries Van Noten, Paul Smith, and Issey Miyake.

The destructured Japanese style took to the street, its followers no longer being limited to a designer "happy few." Lastly, the jacket, that barometer of style, is now seen as ripe for exploration: re-cut, narrow-fitting, double-breasted, asymmetrical, or wrap-around, with contrasting sleeves, collar removed or floating, frayed edges—a vast range of styles reminiscent of the female wardrobe. Designers such as Raf Simons and Dries Van Noten provide ample illustration, and their example is followed in understated models by classic labels and from mass-market retailers.

Lastly, and still more so than for women, sports, rock, and hip-hop have all inflected the shift toward more imagination: shiny materials, high-tech fabrics, zippers, and Velcro, colorful patterns, lighter cuts, off-beat combinations—the transformation seems irreversible. And so Hedi Slimane at Dior Homme dared to mix sneakers with his famous slim tux. A milestone in men's fashion: there is a before and an after Slimane. In the seven years from 2000 to 2007, this designer revolutionized the suit, dragging it out of the boardroom: sexy, slender, and knowingly crumpled, the lines close to the body, made a symbol of cold distinction into an erotic icon. Female customers too made a beeline for this sulfurous item.

The expanding male wardrobe has widened its sphere to take in accessories, jewelry, and cosmetics. Just as for women, time-honored role models are being joined by more recent paragons: once there was Clark Gable, Paul Newman, Marcello Mastroianni, Sean Connery, Bryan Ferry, Mick Jagger, and Alain Delon. Now there's Pete Doherty, Puff Daddy, and Kanye West; Jude Law, Vincent Cassel, and Harry Connick Jr.; or George Clooney, Barack Obama, and Bernard-Henri Lévy. So many precursors, so many styles to choose from for the liberated man.

FACING PAGE
FOR EVER AND EVER
Breton striped prints.
Jean Paul Gaultier's
trademark. Paunches
prohibited! With classic
trench in salmon by
English designer
Paul Smith with some
refined details (collar,
shoulders, topstitching).

MENSWEAR

CHARMERS

Not really so very far from Marcello Mastroianni's Italian classicism, a Vivienne Westwood suit is light and airy, cultivating elegance and high humor: the gaiters hover over gingham and polka dot shoes.

FACING PAGE

Today Marcello Mastroianni could sport exactly the same shirt, tie, jacket, and glasses. Only the cigarette looks dated.

SUPREMELY CHIC
Impeccably cut by
Dries Van Noten (in
the image of the
designer himself),
this outfit is the
focus of a host of
minute details and
accessories. Here is
a more fitted line
than the imposing
presence of Cary
Grant, whose
pleated trousers
have lost nothing
of their seductive
potential.

FLOWER WOMAN
Color and good
humor; the twin
credos of Agatha
Ruiz de la Prada.

THEY DARED TO DO IT

It was the 1960s that threw open the floodgates to:

❖ indecency—minis, see-through, stretch

❖ cross-dressing—tuxedos on girls, military jackets, biker jackets

❖ new materials—vinyl, synthetics, high-tech fabrics

❖ anti-prettiness—new proportions, distortions, the unfinished look

Mary Quant's groovy miniskirt
1960

Born in London in 1934, this Englishwoman started out in 1955 with a boutique called Bazaar on the King's Road. Dissatisfied with her stock, she decided to design inexpensive things she would like to wear herself. The year was 1958. Quant had trained as an illustrator and completed a brief internship with a dressmaker. In the 1950s, skirts descended halfway down the leg, the finishing touch to a decorous style entirely in keeping with the times. Showing the knees was out of the question: Chanel decreed it "inelegant." But the younger generation was intent on sloughing off bourgeois propriety and on dressing differently from its parents. Quant kicked things off by shortening hemlines.

In 1960, the contraceptive pill became available in the United States (France would wait until 1967) and the miniskirt became "political." An emblem of liberation, of provocation, even. To shrieks of outrage from the Establishment shocked by such "indecencies," Mary Quant answered ingenuously that a short skirt made it possible for a girl to run for a bus. With an instinctive nose for marketing, in a stroke of genius she baptized her creation the "mini" after her beloved car. Thirty years later, having made her fortune, she would be invited to design interiors for the iconic compact.

This progressive exposure of the legs was not only to transform the female figure but also a woman's way of moving. And her attitude to life: She now could flout the established order. The drive toward female emancipation was well underway and women were militating for their independence. They began to assert their sexual desires—and there was simply no place for their mothers' ungainly stockings and garters beneath a short skirt. Thus the mini also encouraged the wearing of pantyhose.

In Paris, the couturiers Cardin and Courrèges ennobled this sexy line in more linear and structured collections. As for Mary Quant, jubilantly embracing her role as hell-fire liberator, at the end of the decade she went on to invent hot pants, before giving a new lease of life to makeup with an armory of blushes, foundations, and mascaras all emblazoned with her childlike flower logo.

Tight blouses in seersucker by Cacharel
1963

A blouse that clings to the body thanks to seersucker, a cleverly puckered cotton material invented by Jean Bousquet, owner of the Cacharel label. No more ironing with starch. Photographed by Peter Knapp, it appeared on the cover of *Elle*.

Courrèges: Space Age
1965

Women of the 1960s were active, working and driving cars. Elsewhere, there were dreams of going to the moon and science-fiction films played to packed movie houses. André Courrèges was the first to extrapolate the space revolution into haute couture. The shock was palpable. The press spoke of the "Courrèges bomb," while a sneering Chanel lamented the "destruction of woman, transformed into a little girl." Liberating and rejuvenating the female figure with trapezoid dresses, ribbed knitwear catsuits, "parachute" raincoats, and shiny PVC flat boots, he popularized the miniskirt, trousers, pantsuits, pedal-pushers, and short jumpsuits, beguiling customers with futuristic, sexy visions of a woman suddenly totally at ease in her clothes.

Mary Quant created the mini in 1958.

In a tux, just like a man: Yves Saint Laurent

1966

In the 1960s, one would attend a soirée in a long gown or black tie. Permed hairstyles, low necklines hung with pearl necklaces; it would be unthinkable for a lady to parade in pants in the hallowed precincts of an opera house or theater. Yves Saint Laurent was thirty-two years old when he had the brainwave of translating the male tuxedo into the feminine. Four years earlier—in 1962—he had brilliantly adapted the peacoat for his women friends. With his tuxedo, he was the first to perceive the erotic potential of such masculine attire on the body of a woman. For his winter 1966 show he sent out straight-legged pants, a white blouse with a ruffle and a black bow around the neck, a body-hugging jacket, and the essential wide satin belt. The outfit was to be a ready-to-wear hit, but not in haute couture, where tradition still held sway. Subsequently, for some forty years, the couturier was to hone this personal hallmark, sometimes conserving but a single element, interpreting it in skirts, jumpsuits, and even shorts: satin lapel, outseam braid, bowtie, belt. Like a game. Not a single catwalk without a dose of tux. But it is in its classic incarnation, worn over bare skin, that it's at its most "Saint Laurent." And its sexiest.

Paco Rabanne: Technology and geometry

1968

Disks or squares linked by rings, steel scales, chain mail, paper—inventive and eyebrow-raising, Rabanne is a couturier who cannot but be admired. In his creations, models become works of art.

Pierre Cardin: "Cardine" in relief

1968

A dress in synthetic material, part of which is vacuum-molded in cubes or bumps. Sold for 100 French francs, it was worn by, among others, Lauren Bacall. Growing increasingly pop over the years, the couturier worked vinyl into puff dresses, designed geometrically patterned chasubles, and added apertures to Darth Vader-style helmets that predated the character. A new architecture of clothing.

Hang-up-free leather: Studded and sexy with Azzedine Alaïa

1970

He was the first to really treat leather as a fabric. But Alaïa's offer of a small ready-to-wear collection of studded leather to the house of Charles Jourdan in the late 1970s was rebuffed. It would have been ideal for a brand that had never truly found a style. So much the better: instead Alaïa issued his designs under his own name and they went on to become bestsellers. To this day, his preferred material is leather.

Inside-out? Stitches out! Sonia Rykiel

1974

Her favorite piece: the sweater, with which it all began in 1962. Not yet a designer, she dreamed up a short, close-fitting sweater in a quiet gray, but found it impossible to source, even through her husband's Italian-supplied store. The steely Sonia entered into discussions in Venice and ended up obtaining the long-dreamed-of model—though as yet without visible stitching. But Sonia Rykiel had already shown the determination that was to make her the "queen of knit." Relaxed, refined, intelligent; it was her way of making a stand against the alienation of women subjected to the diktats of *la mode*. On opening a first shop in 1968, she coined a new word, "*démode*," a philosophy of a critical bent that adapted trends to the way women were, rather than the reverse. The end result was a feeling of freedom conveyed in a personal style whose presupposition is that the inside of a piece of clothing should be as beautiful as the out. So, no more hem, no more lining, and a sweater run up to be seen inside and out—right way round and inside-out! This brainwave became the forerunner of the arty-crafty tendency of Belgian designers in the 1990s.

At once liberated, highbrow, and a bit of a tease, a Rykiel woman is the image of her designer.

Rykiel also advocates a "made in France" policy, as yet unaffected by delocalization: young French ready-to-wear, imbued with the meticulous handiwork of haute couture, takes care over detail. And in Rykiel, it shows.

Vintage jeans: Marithé + François Girbaud
1975

They were the first to upgrade your basic denim into a luxury wear product. Even better: They grafted on a powerful emotional charge. Hence, just as one appreciates a great vintage wine produced by a particular harvest, climate, and winemaker, so one grows attached to a vintage Girbaud. In their wake, Levi's and Diesel came to understand the benefits to be drawn from collector's editions.

Underwear as outerwear: Chantal Thomass
1976

It was she who freed lingerie from prudishness. Not so long ago, the bra was not manufactured to be seen, it was simply a complex construction that incorporated anything between fifteen and thirty components. Designed uniquely for their technical qualities, the straps, fastening, and edging were hardly stylish. Chantal Thomass had the cheeky idea of using brightly colored satin, adding pretty topstitching, and rethinking flounces, bows, and straps. Better still: she revived a fashion for the basque and garter belt. Her runway shows were explosive, with men attending in droves. Thanks to her, the blouse began to be worn open to show the bra like a piece of jewelry. Her prêt-à-porter features retro corsets, lacing, and frou-frous.

The snap fastener is modern: agnès b.
1979

Of course the pressure stud existed before agnès b., but the designer's talent was to apply it to fine knits, giving a modern zing to the twinset with mother-of-pearl buttons, whose connotations had until then been rather bourgeois, rather Grace Kelly. By giving it an industrial feel, agnès b. turned it into a "basic," which she goes on to renew, season after season, producing models for men and children. An oft-copied hit.

Clothes in tatters: that's chic
1982

In 1982, it was the turn of Japanese designers to hog the limelight in Paris. Many still remember the shock on seeing the Comme des Garçons show (the name alone!), the work of an austere-looking little woman, Rei Kawakubo. The models, pale and down-in-the-mouth, were dressed in black rags. With carpet slippers on their feet, they shuffled forward like automatons. A hobo look that stood traditional chic on its head and shifted the emphasis to emotion and memory: old blankets, old slippers, and materials that age with the wearer. The becoming, the neat, the sexy—all dead and buried! At the same time, Yohji Yamamoto (Rei's boyfriend) and Issey Miyake's deconstructed, unstructured, asymmetric pieces pushed the point home. Not necessarily easy to wear, but furiously avant-garde, they opened the door to the Belgian wave of Martin Margiela, Ann Demeulemeester, Dirk Bikkembergs, and Walter Van Beirendonck, who also sought an alternative to prettiness and classical elegance.

At last. Men in color—thanks to Kenzo
1983

The Japanese designer had been known since 1970 for his multiculturalism, his joyous colored patterns that were a mix and match of West and East. His men's suits were available in saffron, ocher, or apple green, with a printed shirt to match. Surprisingly, men were keen to give it a go. The Japanese creator had lit a fuse that would take,

Thanks to Kenzo, men, too, can wear color.

however, nearly twenty years to explode into a full-fledged style trend. Before Paul Smith, before Dries Van Noten, gentlemen avoided color and it took a long time to train eyes unaccustomed to chromatic nuances. In thrall to the conventions of understatement, they remained fearful, as if by forsaking their reassuring black-gray-navy-brown cocoon they might be forfeiting something of their respectability—or of their power? By providing an ultra-classic cut, Kenzo convinced them to accept colors which, astonishingly, were no longer the unique preserve of women or artistic types.

Moschino sabotage

1983

Hitherto, provocative messages had been limited to T-shirts. The Italian designer, who died prematurely in 1994, applied irony to altogether more upmarket (and dearer) items (though his second line was called Cheap and Chic). His objective: to poke fun at fashion diktats, at the exclusivity of the fashion system. For example, he reworked a Chanel jacket, decorating it with braid and gaudy appliqués; or, on the back of a chic jacket, he inscribed in gold lamé the words "Expensive Jacket"; or "Bull Chic" on a matador-style ensemble. He had fun decorating a traditional blazer with bottle tops. Some of his provocations earned him lawsuits—on behalf of Chanel and Vuitton, in particular.

Jean Paul Gaultier puts men in skirts

1985

Madcap gender-bending pioneer Gaultier, in his "wardrobe for two" runway show, infamously presented a long skirt for men, as dapper as any suit. Rei Kawakubo for Comme des Garçons and Yohji Yamamoto proposed further versions. Among their customers: Marc Jacobs, who made it part of his own wardrobe. Since 2007 the pressure group Men in Skirts has taken up the cry loud and clear, but general acceptance remains far off. As Sean Connery puts it: "A man in a kilt who's not a Scot is in the end just a man in a skirt."

Xuly Bët: sexy-recycled-street style

1986

This African designer—mother from Senegal, father from Mali—launched accessible fashion based on recycled clothing and stretch fabrics. His credo: to emphasize feminine curves with skintight dresses, long or mini, graffiti prints, and bright colors. In his little workshop, with few means, he "bones" stockings, net T-shirts, and stuff from markets, turning them into clothing worn as overlays. Sequins, inserts, unlined jackets, visible stitching in contrasting colors and a humorous red logo. Funk Fashion is born. A push to "street style." He has collaborated with the 3 Suisses mail-order catalog, Puma, the Leclerc supermarket, and launched a fair-trade cotton company in Mali.

Nike: sneakers on a cushion of air

1987

Mounted on compressed air, Air Max sneakers were invented for Nike by the designer Tinker Hatfield. A revolutionary style that was inspired by Renzo Piano's Pompidou Center in Paris, a building that exposes its technical infrastructure instead of hiding it. Here, it's the air cushion on which the shoe is built that appears along the sole. Over the years, the visible line of the air cushion altered. The sneakers became a true urban icon, a sign of recognition for rappers and a favorite (in the eyes of the British police) with underage English criminals.

Xuly Bët gives stretch mesh and tie-dye a "couture" touch.

Marie Mercié gives the hat a new lease on life

1987

The hat had previously been the preserve of retro grannies at well-heeled weddings, duchesses at the races, and the Queen of England. With Marie Mercié, the hat returned to fashion. But much more fun. Her unhinged imagination reduced the rules and regulations to smithereens. From simple pillbox to wide-brimmed hat, it is a garment that can tell stories, performing elaborate sketches starring fish and forests, birds, and idealized landscapes—and even an upside-down couch. She redesigned its lines, too, modernizing and restyling them to the nth degree—with curves, waves, haloes, spirals, or giant arabesques. A whole profession is reborn, blazing the way for Philip Treacy, Jean-Charles Brosseau, and many others. It was not long before the men were at it: in 2000, Anthony Peto, an associate of Marie Mercié's, re-imagined the panama, and guys went wild for it. A trend destined to last, spurred on by the adoption of color in the male closet.

The French exoticism of Christian Lacroix

1988

Inspiration had long been sought in remote places: Russia, India, China, Africa, but Christian Lacroix got it into his head to draw on the folklore of Arles! The world of fashion, from New York to Tokyo, remained slack-jawed before such baroque profusion, an insane mix of religious imagery, bullfighting, and Provençal and gypsy traditions. For over twenty years, this once isolated region in the south of France, between Arles and the Camargue, has remained a fertile source of fantasy and ecstasy.

With Jean-Claude Jitrois, no more baggy leather

1989

To prevent leather creasing and sagging, Jitrois had the bright idea of elasticating it with a thin coat of stretch cotton. Result: lambskin, suede, and then python (in 2006) morph into genuine "second skins." Taking this method further, Jitrois came up with a way of making the material change color as it stretches: the result was Stretch Hallu leather (1998). In 2002, he launched smocked leather before, in 2009, announcing the arrival of machine-washable leather jeans.

Alexander McQueen's low-cut jeans

1993

As anarchic as they are inventive, as provocative as they are contrived, in less than twenty years Alexander McQueen's runway happenings accumulated enough political capital to make even the most radical of contemporary art lovers blanch. Starting with jeans cut so low that they show the top of the buttocks. He called them the "bumster," conscious of the controversy they were sure to ignite. The bumster was enthusiastically taken up by the young of the entire planet, from thugs to daddies' boys. Then came his polemical Highland Rape collection, with models dressed as battered women, dresses spattered with blood, and the runway show with Aimee Mullins, a double amputee perched on carved wood prosthetic legs; there was also the psychiatric hospital show, with girls disguised as madwomen, one with a rat on her shoulder, another bedecked in Hitchcock's crows, and finishing with a naked obese model surrounded by cockroaches. Not forgetting the "mechanical doll" show at which a model took to the catwalk hobbled by a metal cage. In short, attending his shows was to live through an uncompromising artistic and political experience. With him fashion flirted with artistic tragedy.

Christian Lacroix at his final show keeps faith with his references, from the Madonna of Arles to black: passions from the South.

Hussein Chalayan hits out with the chador

1997

This provocative English designer of Turkish-Cypriot origin and graduate of Central Saint Martins in London explored the chador in his 1998 spring-summer collection. A daring statement when one is called Hussein, after the sacred imam. He was twenty-seven and decided to send his final six models down the runway partially clothed in a burqa with shorter and shorter hems, climbing to the waist and showing the pubis, and then the whole body—but with the face remaining concealed. "A way of illustrating the loss of identity," he explained simply. Recognized for his avant-garde work and for pursuing his experimentation with clothing, after the turn of the millennium he began investigating the value of new technologies applied to fabric.

With Alicia Framis, fashion takes up a political position

2002

The Spanish artist Alicia Framis created a manifesto against racism and violence: her Anti-Dog collection features twenty-three dresses manufactured out of Twaron, a bullet-, stab-, and bite-proof fabric. The models aped the lines of Dior, Courrèges, or Gaultier, but were emblazoned with provocative slogans: "Fuck you," "Go back to where you belong." This disconcerting collection was shown in Paris, Barcelona, Madrid, Helsingborg, Sweden, Birmingham, in the surrounds of an Amsterdam stadium, and at other tough urban venues.

Smart textiles: Élisabeth de Senneville

2003

Everyone has heard of antiperspirant and odor-eating fabrics. Moisturizing pantyhose even. This designer has produced prototypes of which dreams are made: a garment lined with silver wire to deflect electromagnetic waves from cell phones; liquid crystals integrated into the collar and sleeves which, via fiber optics, store daylight and release it at night. Opening new perspectives, she collaborates closely with research laboratories and industrialists. The Textronics company sells an intelligent sports bra that monitors heart-rate. Designer Ellie Gosse creates anti-microbial fiber clothing for dogs to combat parasites. Other researchers have invented solar-harvesting fabrics that produce electricity so wearers can recharge their cell phones. And in case you were wondering how it can be washed, the encapsulation occurs in the dye itself: "functional," i.e., conducting, lines transport current or information.

Vuitton: art and global luxury

2003

The venerable luggagemaker, which dates back to 1854 and whose monogrammed canvas is a bourgeois stalwart, chose Takashi Murakami, the manga artist, to decorate its bags: cherries, jellyfish eyes, acid colors. It was the first time that an artist could bask in the global reach of a luxury brand—one that subsequently sponsored his shows, setting up temporary boutiques in the exhibition hall.

Karl Lagerfeld takes on the mass market

2011

In late 2010, the most iconic personality in the world of luxury made an enormous stir by announcing that he was to transform his own label, Karl Lagerfeld, into an affordably priced mass-market brand, and, what's more, sell it on the Internet. This wasn't just a capsule collection for H&M. Here, mass production and prestige would go hand in hand.

A luminous dress in experimental fabric by Hussein Chalayan: the thread is interlaced with fiber optics.

MILITARY PRECISION
The celebrated
Tank watch, invented
by Louis Cartier.
Fascinated by
the tanks on
the battlefields
of World War I,
Cartier paid them
an unusual homage.
Taking inspiration
from their shape
as seen from above,
his watch forms
a square flanked by
two lugs resembling
caterpillar tracks.
Made in platinum,
the first Tank was
sold on November 12,
1919, one year after
the Armistice,
as Cartier did not
want to put the
item on the market
before peace was
restored. Since
then, the model
has evolved,
but its characteristics
remain unchanged:
Roman numerals
for the hours (and
IIII for four o'clock,
instead of IV), hands
in the form of
a swordblade,
"railroad" minute
track, and
a winder tipped
with a sapphire.

1675

The king offers patents to dressmakers: Women blaze the trail

By royal decree, Louis XIV granted mistress-dressmakers the right to dress women and children—but not men! Not only did this open a market for clothes to social classes beyond the nobility; it also afforded these tradeswomen a measure of independence, even potentially setting them up as rivals to the all-powerful clothiers whose modest assistants they had previously been. A century later, the *modiste* Rose Bertin opened an emporium, Le Grand Mogol, and became Queen Marie-Antoinette's favorite dressmaker and then her unofficial "minister for fashion," thereby inaugurating the onset of France's sartorial dominance over every court in Europe.

1824

The first department stores selling off-the-rack clothes: fashion becomes democratic

La Belle Jardinière was first off the starting blocks in Paris and soon branches were springing up in the provinces. Other names saw the light of day, each offering a shop-window on modernity: Le Bon Marché in 1852; Les Grands Magasins du Louvre in 1855; Printemps in 1865; La Samaritaine in 1870; and Galeries Lafayette (once a notions store), in 1895, expanding into its present-day setting by 1912. In London, that summit of class, Harrods, was inaugurated in 1849, and was soon frequented by prestigious customers, beginning with the queen herself, but also Oscar Wilde, Sigmund Freud, and Alfred Hitchcock. In New York, in 1901, the business kicked off with Bergdorf Goodman, founded by Herman Bergdorf in association with Edwin Goodman in 1906. The firm grew into a sumptuous temple of deluxe consumerism, to be followed by a host of others: Neiman Marcus, Macy's, Gimbels, Saks Fifth Avenue, and Marshall Field's.

1830

Barthélemy Thimmonier's incredible sewing machine

For the first time replacing sewing by hand with a machine (from 30 to 200 stitches a minute) became feasible. At first this invention was sabotaged by furious tailors fearful for their jobs. Success came only in 1849, when the inventor went to manufacture his machines in Manchester, England. With a passion, Thimonnier continued to improve his invention, adding backstitch, lockstitch, novelty stitches, and so on. Industrialization was underway.

1892

Birth of the magazine *Vogue*, then *Marie Claire*, then *Elle*: women's liberation as fun

Founded by Arthur Baldwin Turnure and taken over at his death in 1909 by Condé Nast, the fashion and trend bible *Vogue* was initially a weekly magazine, then a bimonthly, before becoming a monthly. From the 1910s, Nast exported the concept to Europe, beginning in England. Today there exist some eighteen editions. Well before its American editor in chief Anna Wintour arrived in 1988 (she features in the documentary *The September Issue* and the move *The Devil Wears Prada*), *Vogue*, piloted by its editor Diana Vreeland, took up daring positions on social phenomena. In its glossy and chic pages in the 1960s, for example, there was much talk of women's lib and sexual revolution. Since then, economic realism and a tried-and-tested formula of fun and frolics have toned things down: the fashions peddled by advertisers and a handful of young designers are given all the plaudits.

Meanwhile, in France in 1937, Jean Prouvost took his cue from the American market and founded *Marie Claire*, a magazine that now has nearly thirty international editions. In the beginning, the then weekly was perceived by the clergy as "a threat to chastity and faithfulness," because, open to American influences, it dealt with women's liberation and social ascendency. Just after the war in 1945 came *Elle*, founded by a couple, Pierre Lazareff and his wife Hélène Gordon, who had cut her teeth in the United States at *Marie Claire*. Its bywords were "seriousness in frivolity and irony in earnestness." The glossy (now appearing in thirty international editions) remained through the decades an unchallenged arbiter of trends, while still championing the cause of women.

People visit Harrods department store in London as they would an historic building, especially the escalators now restored to their original 1930s Egyptian style.

1929

The French sell their ideas to the United States

The year 1929 saw the stock market crash that sparked the Great Depression. Couture houses and the textile industry in general suffered the inevitable consequences. To protect its threatened clothes sector, the US government decided to tax imported clothing but left patterns (the structure of the piece cut out and squared up on paper) and toiles (test garments run up in white cotton) exempt from duty. In this manner, French couturiers were obliged, if they did not want to sacrifice the American market entirely, to sell their creations to industrialists, who—heresy!—would copy them and subject them to mass production.

1931-35

Mainbocher, Schiaparelli, Balenciaga... the whole world comes to Paris

Right in the middle of a full-blown economic slump, the American Main Rousseau Bocher (a native of Chicago and editor in chief of French *Vogue*) suddenly decided to set up his own couture house. And it worked: his strict-looking dresses, the waist highlighted by a corset, would be worn by aristocrats and the jetset (in 1937 he made the Duchess of Windsor's wedding dress). That same year, the Italian Elsa Schiaparelli opened a shop for her surrealist creations on place Vendôme and the Spaniard Cristóbal Balenciaga fled the Civil War to settle near the Champs-Élysées, becoming one of the most outstanding personalities in fashion. Paris has always attracted foreign designers.

1940

The first nylon stockings

Previously, stockings had been made of silk imported from Japan, an expensive and fragile product. In 1938, the scientist Wallace Hume Carothers at the American firm of DuPont de Nemours invented a new polymer, a filamentous paste of whitish color which, when cooled, became elastic and resistant. This in turn gave rise to neoprene (advantageously used as ersatz rubber during the War) and nylon. May 15, 1940 saw the first countrywide sale of nylon stockings: "N-Day" prices were twice those of silk

stockings, but the nylons were longer lasting and sheerer. The GIs who entered Paris at the Liberation in 1945 introduced them to the French. In 1952, Bernard Gilberstein, owner of a weaving company, exploited the potential of nylon by simplifying manufacture and inventing the seamless stocking in 1956, launching the Bas Dimanche. In 1968, rechristened Dim, the brand launched Tels Quels pantyhose. The year 2007 saw a minisociological revolution: in response to increasing demand, the Gerbe brand brought out the first pantyhose for men, with a fly and a very broad knitted waistband.

1954

At seventy-one, Mademoiselle Chanel imposes her own brand of chic

Coco Chanel had quit the fashion scene fifteen years previously, after streamlining and "androgynizing" the female silhouette since 1910. Recalled to design by Wertheimer, the owners of her label, the old lady won back customers by inventing a braid-trimmed tweed suit worn over a silk blouse and given a feminine touch by a cascade of pearls. A timeless style was born.

1958

Yves Saint Laurent comes out of nowhere

After his untimely death, Christian Dior was succeeded by a shy young man of twenty-one who was to turn the codes of the New Look then de rigueur in the great fashion house upside-down: his first collection, Trapèze, loosened the waist. "I never saw a better Dior collection," Eugenia Sheppard was to write in the *Herald Tribune*. A year later, in association with Pierre Bergé, the couturier set up his own house.

1959

Lycra... bold and sexy

In the beginning, it was called elastane or spandex (an anagram of "expands"). It is a synthetic material derived from polyurethane, an organic molecule developed by the scientist Joseph C. Shivers of DuPont after a ten-year research program. Whereas latex tapped from the rubber tree, being less durable and sometimes allergenic,

January 30, 1958. Yves Saint Laurent surrounded by his models presents the Trapèze collection at Dior.

Lycra went on to revolutionize the clothing industry. Highly elastic, the fiber can resist being stretched by up to 600 percent before breaking. In its first ten years, Lycra was taken up by athletes—cyclists, gymnasts, dancers—before entering ready-to-wear in the guise of skintight clothing. Its unrestrained use put some backs up: "Lycra means you'll never have to learn how to cut," thundered the austere Cristóbal Balenciaga. He was right: the inexpensive clothing industry leapt on this light, crush-proof product, easy to dye, pleasant to the touch, simplifying cutting to absurdity. It took about thirty years to learn the right proportion of Lycra to add to a fabric.

1967
Summer of Love: the hippie style is born

Taking off in the early 1960s in California, the hippie movement reached its peak in San Francisco, at Golden Gate Park, near Haight-Ashbury, where free concerts were held. That summer of 1967, it could be seen everywhere, both on stage and off where people smoked dope and made love. Strange battalions of androgynous creatures wandered here and there, bare feet in sandals, their locks adorned with straggly hairbands, in colorful embroidered tunics, Afghan vests, bell-bottom jeans customized with shells and flowers, with jangling Indian bracelets and necklaces, and exhaling the heady aroma of patchouli. The exoticism of the time was soon contesting the formal austerity of the Western wardrobe. Twenty years later, designers were to plunge deep into these features for inspiration. Flower Power, psychedelic patterns derived from LSD trips, fringes, rhinestone, layers of silk, and "ethnic" necklaces—the hippie chic style became a classic.

1968
The H&M "revolution": here today, gone tomorrow

In the beginning, there was Hennes (Swedish for "hers"), whose first shop was opened in Vasteras, Sweden, in 1947 by Erling Persson on his return from a trip to America. The goal: to make purchasing fashion less daunting and less expensive, to enable impulse buys that would be quickly forgotten. In 1968, he bought out the Mauritz Widforss stores, redesigning the whole as a chain for women and men, and then for children. In 1982, his son, Stefan Persson, picked up the torch, followed by grandson Carl-Johan. By the late 1980s, the chain expanded internationally abroad. Its secret? A trend bureau that keeps tabs on what's out there and reacts super quickly—whether this means "copying" designer items or replicating a star's latest outfit—outsourcing to countries with cheap labor, and constantly monitoring sales to adjust stocks. Press campaigns with headline personalities—Claudia Schiffer, Cindy Crawford—were added to prevent its being labeled as "downmarket." After opening in Britain, 1998 saw H&M launch outlets in France.

1969
Gap fills a gap

A real estate agent in San Francisco, Donald Fisher, and his wife Doris, couldn't find the right "casual wear" on the retail market: simple pants, natural fabrics, wool, cotton, jeans, in uncomplicated colors, navy, beige, khaki, white. So they launched a range based on quality, practicality, and simplicity and soon Gap—the one between the generations!—took off, soon adding GapKids and BabyGap, not to mention maternity and lingerie lines. It has become a textile group, with Old Navy and Banana Republic. Sharon Stone turns up at the Oscars in a Gap turtleneck and all swear by their classic white shirts: like Ralph Lauren sportswear, but less to fork out. Until 2000 that is: reacting to a collapse in sales, the firm widened its scope without jettisoning its trademark plain palette. Prints, the odd flounce, brighter colors, and some understated models drawn by a voguish designer (but not signed) once again catch the eye of fashion cruisers. Without being at the top of the hit parade, Gap, with some 3,000 outlets worldwide, remains a classic, if one whose style is slightly nondescript.

1975
Armani jacket? Na, Zara!

Amancio Ortega opened the first Zara store in La Coruña in Spain. The name, Zara, comes apparently from the town of Zadar. The concept: to copy emblematic models by great couture houses, altering the details to stay on the right side of the counterfeit law, sell the same range the world over, and never to restock, but constantly renew

Make love not war! A 1970s ad for an Ossie Clark dress, a flower-power model that has scarcely dated.

the collection thanks to a vast style bureau with its ear firmly to the ground. Fine fabrics, carefully cut, good finishing, variety—for the first time the general public could have the impression of buying almost couture.

1982

"*Jeunes créateurs*" against the Japanese!

In one corner, Mugler, Montana, Alaïa, and Gaultier, who, each in his own manner, revolutionized fashion with revisited sex appeal, embraced by future supermodels like Naomi Campbell, Cindy Crawford, and Linda Evangelista. And in the other, the hair-raising apparitions of two subversive Japanese designers: Rei Kawakubo for Comme des Garçons and Yohji Yamamoto. On their runways, wan-faced models traipse along in silence, wearing slippers and haphazardly draped tattered "rags," the whole body submerged in expanses of rough-looking black.

A clash between two visions of fashion: the "hobo"—a return to the sources that rejects eroticism and adornment—and a bad-girl, spunky, punk-rock femininity. Between these two camps, another Japanese designer dealt in poetry composed of fabric—layered, asymmetric and permanently creased: Issey Miyake. New visions, all destined to become benchmarks.

1983

Karl Lagerfeld, future emperor of fashion

Gabrielle Chanel died in 1971, still at work at the age of eighty-seven. After her, the house drifted until Alain Wertheimer came to the rescue, convincing Karl Lagerfeld to leave Chloé and come to Chanel. The designer modernized brilliantly the artistic heritage of the house without betraying it, tirelessly reinterpreting and enriching its DNA: the iconic suit, the little black dress, accessories. During his reign, Chanel acquired global exposure without losing its elitism. A global star, he is now just known as Karl.

1984

The runway as showbiz

To celebrate ten years at the house, the flamboyant Thierry Mugler took over the Zénith in Paris for a true "catwalk show": 350 models performed on the theme "the winter of the angels" before professionals *and* a general audience numbering some 6,000 who had to buy a ticket as if for a rock concert. Until the mid-1960s, the atmosphere around the runways was muted, measured, and the houses would unveil their models in plushly decorated showrooms. Then, as if in a futuristic utopia, Courrèges had his models dance, while in 1971 Kenzo invaded a small performance hall for an energetic shindig, which, however, was savored solely by trade journalists and buyers. In Tokyo in 1974, Issey Miyake presented his collection in front of 8,000 people: Issey with Kansai. These "shows" were to become events in 1980s, before returning to more traditional, less outlandish incarnations in the 2000s.

1985

After United Colors of Benetton, advertising will never be the same again

Piloted by the Eldorado advertising agency, the multicolored sweater chain found its slogan. Soon its ad campaigns were being scrutinized as a barometer of social change. Based on the colors (of the sweaters!), the photos on the posters played the multiracial card. Gradually the product receded to just leave the message. Each of Oliviero Toscani's images seemed to symbolize peace and tolerance. Religion, homosexuality, AIDS—as the topics widened, the furore intensified. The breach opened, other no less shocking campaigns followed, even for the luxury market, in a porn chic or transgender vein.

1990

A minimalist offensive from the North

They have little in common—except their desire for clarity, for deconstruction. The Belgians Martin Margiela, Ann Demeulemeester, the couple A. F. Vandevorst (An and Filip), the Austrian Helmut Lang, the German Jil Sander, the Franco-Swede Marcel Marongiu have all fueled a backlash against the extravagance of the 1980s and 1990s:

Ines de la Fressange on the catwalk in Castelbajac with a nod to Andy Warhol. Since 1984, the designer who loves artists has been laying the foundations of a genuine collaboration between art and fashion.

reduced palettes, emphasis on materials, original if still classic lines—each in their own manner contesting the fashion-style treadmill and advocating an expressionist, artistic, committed approach in clothing that says "no": no to logos, to artifice, to vulgarity. The initial stirrings of ecological awareness.

1994
Anglo-Saxon marketing serves a wake-up call to European labels

Domenico de Sole, the chairman of the venerable Italian leathermakers Gucci, decided to appoint the American Tom Ford as creative director. In ten years, the label skyrocketed to become one of the most ebullient emblems of the 1990s. From 1993 to 2002, the flawlessly elegant Oscar de la Renta, an American designer of Dominican origin, shook up Lanvin rather more discreetly. By 1997, Marc Jacobs was doing the same for Vuitton. The recipe: identify the customer base; target and adapt models to that market. It's called marketing. In 1996, two young English talents were taken on by LVMH to rejuvenate a pair of legendary labels: John Galliano at Givenchy from 1995 to 1996, before being summoned to Dior and Alexander McQueen at Givenchy for five years from 1995 to 2001. Both gave a new lease on life to the venerable French houses.

1999-2000
The Best of American casual

After the golden age of Hollywood glamour and its designers in the 1930s and 1940s, the Americans seemed to take a back seat. This style, a little too focused on the practical, the comfortable, and the versatile (in other words, somewhat impersonal), has been slightly disdained in Europe, even if a style-conscious wardrobe probably contains a Calvin Klein shirt, a Donna Karan bodysuit, a Ralph Lauren cardigan, a Diane von Furstenberg dress, or a Michael Kors bag (see his interesting work for Céline from 1997 to 2003).

After the "hangover" of the 1980s, we started to appreciate sobriety, simplicity, and wearability. Without going as far as the concept clothing of the Japanese or Belgian designers, these famous Americans bring a laid-back,

uncomplicated charm. Now Narciso Rodriguez, Thakoon, Derek Lam, and Proenza Schouler are taking the baton; each offers an originality of their own without being megalomaniac.

2004
Karl Lagerfeld at H&M: designer labels for every pocket

H&M was the first clothing chain to grasp the need to cultivate elitism in the mass market. The inexpensive Swedish brand called on major couturiers, soliciting capsule collections that their customers fought for. Other chains followed in their wake: New Look, Top Shop, Mango, and Etam all signed contracts with up-and-coming young talents in an effort to personalize their collections.

2007
India hits the scene

Manish Arora, Ana Mika, and Rajesh Pratap were introduced to the Parisian fashion show calendar. Paris was enchanted. Three years later, Manish Arora was to design half a dozen shimmering delights for the mail-order catalog, La Redoute.

2009
Christian Lacroix goes bust

After more than twenty years of haute couture and prêt-à-porter, the house filed for bankruptcy. This is a powerful symbol of French fashion on the rocks: exuberance, flamboyance, lyricism, and a certain indifference to the demands of marketing. The designer continues to collaborate, solo, on theater and opera projects.

2010
The suicide of Alexander McQueen

The brilliant English bad boy of fashion committed suicide in his home one February morning, leaving an unfinished collection hailed by all and proof that the art of fashion can be a fatal obsession.

Manish Arora, an Indian couturier whose imagination, sparkling kitsch, and talent as a colorist have conquered Paris.

VIBRANT
Scarf by Danish
designer Bess
Nielsen for Épice.
The shades of its
wool voile weave
resemble the
faded, washed
look characteristic
of Scandinavian
design.

9

30 DESIGNERS

AGNÈS B.

Her style

She launched a highly Parisian relaxed chic look in tandem with the concept of the "basic." Her favorite colors: white, black, gray for all (even for children, to avoid cutesiness). For years she has been renewing "permanents," from ever-fashionable well-cut black pants to white shirts. There's nothing sexless about her outfits, however: they're fresh, feminine, though with little ornament. Carefully targeted by demographic, the brand dresses the style-conscious with an eye for color and arty graphics, those who like any color as long as it's black, and fans of natural fibers or natty 1950s frocks. The cardigan with its trademark pearly pressure studs is now rebranded as a dress and even a swimsuit. Agnès b. is alive to trends, but likes to keep them at arm's length. For men, in addition to her classics, relaxed jackets and lightweight, dark shirts, she plays readily with ironic patterns. Customers can shop with their eyes closed, sure, above and beyond the trends, to find what they need. She hasn't pushed the green policy to the point of eschewing leather: her coats and jackets are classics. We hardly need to add that on the podium she avoids skinny models, preferring "real people."

Who is she?

A small, fair woman of unassuming appearance, she stands at the head of a vast empire. Born in 1941 in Versailles, she went to art school and started out as a fashion writer on the magazine *Elle* before turning to design and entering into apprenticeships with Dorothée Bis, VdeV, and Pierre d'Alby. She set up her own label in 1973, opening her first shop two years later. The "b." of her label comes from her first husband, the publisher Christian Bourgois, who passed away in 2007. The success of her timeless, accessibly priced, and easy-to-wear style, much influenced by her travels, was immediate. In 1979, she invented her famous snap cardigan, still available today. This hit opened the doors to America and to New York, where the graffiti proved a great inspiration. She became the first to ask taggers to illustrate T-shirts. In 1981, she launched a menswear line, then a children's collection, followed by cosmetics and luggage. In 1984, thanks to her prosperous brand—and without much in the way of a publicity campaign—Agnès joined the ranks of fashion patrons and opened her first art gallery, starting out showing photographers and graffiti artists. In the 1990s, she launched into movie production, supporting rock and rap artists, and publishing the review *Point d'ironie*, each issue of which is devoted to a particular artist. She has also worked with various foundations in the fight against AIDS and in favor of women's and children's rights. She has also tried to ensure that the label remains "made in France," and taken up the green agenda with biodegradable bags made of potato starch for her boutiques.

"I tend to mix the emotions of a human, mystical, and aesthetic nature."

AZZEDINE ALAÏA

Who is he?

This Tunisian always clad in black, espadrilles, and Mao jacket is famous for his intransigent personality and outspokenness. This is worth mentioning as it's pretty rare in fashion. There's practically only Karl Lagerfeld—whom he cordially loathes—to give him his own back! Like Karl, he carefully conceals his year of birth. 1940? 1939? 1938? "Age, it's in the head!", he rightly barks. He studied sculpture in the art school in Tunis, sewing with his sister, worked with a dressmaker to finance his studies, and pored over the pages of *Vogue*. He left Tunisia for Paris in the 1950s, where he was taken on at Dior. "Five days sewing labels!" With his temperament, he soon upped sticks and joined Guy Laroche, where he spent two seasons refining his technique.

In 1960, the aristocratic Blegiers family took him on as their estate steward and dressmaker to the countess (and her friends). While working in parallel for other brands, he caught the eye of Parisian high society, meeting actress Arletty and writer Louise de Vilmorin, who were to remain models of femininity in his mind forever with their blend of cheek and elegant fantasy. His customers remained faithful to him when, in 1970s, he founded a label of his own, working out of his small apartment. More than forty years later, he remains a craftsman through and through, keen on establishing personal relationships with his clients. Copied and very much in demand among some of the best-known women in the world—from Naomi Campbell to Grace Jones and Michelle Obama—he has never indulged in megalomania. When in 2000 Prada proposed a "marriage" to finance wider development—accessories, diffusion lines, sales outlets—the union was to last for seven years. Today, he is financially associated with the Swiss group Richemont and continues to present in his showroom in the Marais according to a mysterious calendar known only to himself, master in his own kingdom.

His style

Alaïa has a way with feminine curves. Whether in knit viscose dresses, peplum jackets, or fine wool crepe redingotes, he manages to pour the garment over the body like a second skin. With bias-cut, astutely placed seams, openings, and piping, he makes the most of the body shape. The art of cutting: apparently simple, but so hard to pull off. You can be wafer thin, in his figure-hugging dresses you'll soon acquire curves. If you feel too plump, the sex appeal of Alaïa's work is so undeniable that it'll soon make you feel better about yourself. His knitwear—made in Italy, like his shoes—is the result of tireless experimentation: jersey, ribbed, openwork, rippling or stiff, swirling or in stretch bands, it "holds" the body like a sheath, like a surgeon's lancet that knows exactly where to cut and where to inject. The materials shimmer iridescently or revel in deep colors. Moreover, if the couturier delights in sexy lines, he only believes in classic hues: black and white especially, plain beige, gray, and red. Another Alaïa "basic": bright, white cotton shirts. Lastly, his other favorite material is leather—of reptiles especially, crocodile, python, lizard—which he handles better than anyone: sensual jackets and coats, short blousons perched on low necklines. As he has stated loud and clear: there's no question of forsaking models patiently constructed over the years and adored by his clients. He reworks and revisits them with no more than subtle changes in proportion. One of a kind, Alaïa sees no difference between haute couture and prêt-à-porter. Neither, alas, does his pricing policy.

"I prefer intelligent bodies to beautiful bodies. Certain gorgeous girls have no piquancy; on the contrary, others, less beautiful, are as jumpy as racehorses. One also meets girls without much of a figure who look unbelievable in a dress."

GIORGIO ARMANI

Who is he?

He has been dubbed the father of Italian fashion. But he's much more than that. Armani has created an empire with fingers in every sector of the lifestyle industry pie: in addition to eight prêt-à-porter lines, haute couture, and innumerable accessories and cosmetics, he has launched a furniture collection, designed hotels, as well as a score of cafés and restaurants throughout the world. His Milan catwalk shows are organized in his very own theater. Add three or four second homes, such as the oft-photographed one on Pantelleria, a jewel of modern seaside architecture where he receives his Hollywood chums. In short, for a young man who lived through the devastation of war and dreamed of becoming a doctor (he studied for two years at college), he has—economically at least—been a huge success. He was born in Piacenza in 1934 and initially trained in menswear with Nino Cerruti. It was with his friend Sergio Galeotti that he founded his initially exclusively male prêt-à-porter house in 1974. Together they formed a complementary management–design tandem, the secret of the label's longevity. Fifteen years of expansion and diversification followed. In 1985, Galeotti died of a heart attack. But Armani still gets up at seven, spending an hour and a half in the gym before heading off to the office. Today, there's no red-carpet event without an Armani dress.

His style

One word sums up Armani elegance: fluidity. Fluid materials, crisp wool, linen, silk, loose lines, and destructured jackets without shoulder pads, sometimes without linings. He has also been able to adapt the severity of the male cut to women's wear. And conversely, he affords men a soft, relaxed look more in keeping with the fall of a woman's garment. Lightly draped, wide, shawl collars, understated slit pockets, slimline cuts, Mao cuts and just the right length to camouflage flaws. It's also that feel for "real world" vital statistics that has made him so successful with American customers. Moreover, he was one of the first to ban ultra-thin models from his catwalk shows. His color scheme has become a benchmark: every shade of beige, ecru, charcoal gray, navy blue, denim, off-white. He applies touches of bright color and graphic lines in relief. His evening dresses for more spectacular events boast rhinestone inlays, gleaming embroidery, geometric patterns in jet: a well-balanced sensuality.

"One can always learn how to have fun, to have a good time. But for me it's too late. I've always worked, I can't do anything else."

NICOLAS GHESQUIÈRE FOR BALENCIAGA

His style

It derives from his personal flair, sense of proportion, and a movie culture nourished by science fiction from *Star Wars* to *Logan's Run*. In fact, his collections can be recognized because of a vaguely *Fifth Element* futurism mitigated by an eminently Balenciaga sense of volume. It should be remembered that the master was a brilliant tailor with a passion for ample volumes. The Balenciaga exhibition in the Musée de la Mode in Paris in 2006–07 showed dazzling virtuosity in cut and assembly, turning dresses and coats into majestically curved sculptures. Ghesquière takes up the idea and modernizes it: some dresses skim the body, holding only on to the curves. His style is varied, but he often returns to black, gray, bias cuts, folds, and abstract prints. No froufrous and no camber. Rigor, geometry, sobriety.

Who is he?

In the beginning, this star designer was no Parisian inspired by trends and hip shopping jaunts. He was born in the provinces, in 1971 in the Pas-de-Calais, a mining and rural region where fashion is not the chief concern. His father owned a golf club and his mother would buy fashion magazines. Ghesquière, too, liked clothing and did an internship with agnès b. and then with Corinne Cobson, aged just fourteen. Central Saint Martin's or Studio Berçot were not for him; he learned on the job, in particular with Jean Paul Gaultier, becoming one of his assistants after leaving high school. He stayed on from 1990 to 1992, before moving on to knitwear with Thierry Mugler, shoes with Stephane Kélian, and leather with Trussardi. Entering Balenciaga by the backdoor working for the Asian market, he made a splash with a collection of uniforms for Japan.

Then, when he was just twenty-six, the PPR Group offered him the position of creative director, a shock decision whose aim was to shake up a house that had fallen by the wayside since the death of its Spanish founder Cristóbal Balenciaga. In four years, the young designer had given the label back its bite and it took off again. Chloë Sevigny became a fan, as did Nicole Kidman and the Olsen sisters, and especially the shy Charlotte Gainsbourg, who became the face for the fragrance line in 2010.

"Traditional haute couture is finished. One has to channel one's know-how into ready-to-wear."

JEAN-CHARLES DE CASTELBAJAC

Who is he?

He is the most aristocratic of designers, and the most non-conformist. From his Catholic education (from age six to seventeen) with the Oratorians and the Brothers of Bétharram, he seems to have retained a taste for transgression. His taste for fashion comes from his mother, Jeanne-Blanche, Marquise de Castelbajac (née Empereur-Bissonet), founder of the boutique Ko & Co. in Limoges. Study at art school and at the Higher School of the Clothing Industry provided him with a solid artistic and technical grounding. He launched his first collection in 1969. His noble ancestors back in Bigorre must have been turning in their graves: the youngster of the family was using floor-cloths, sponges, and oilcloth to make clothes. In 1973, it was the turn of Ace bandages, protective nylon, and mica visors. *Women's Wear Daily* was ecstatic, hailing him as a new Courrèges. He brought out the first down coat; a two-person poncho; and designed costumes for the theater and the cinema. In 1976, he dreamed up Farrah Fawcett's garb for the series *Charlie's Angels*. He set up his own label in 1979 and, a collector himself, learned a lot from his encounters with artists. By 1982, he was showing dress-cum-paintings illustrated by his friends Jean-Charles Blais, Gérard Garouste, Hervé Di Rosa, Miquel Barceló, and making a series of tributes to Mapplethorpe, Basquiat, Cindy Sherman, Andy Warhol, the Sex Pistols, and even Mickey Mouse. In 1984, he waded in with oversize Gulliver dresses, then dresses with an accumulation of gloves, socks, teddy bears. A man of many interests, he has collaborated with industry, including Air France, the K-Way company, and the furniture compagny Ligne Roset. In 1992, he created a furniture and elegant dining line; in 1997, vestments for Pope Jean Paul II and 5,500 ecclesiastics.

Commercially, his label had its ups and downs. Hyperactive and party-going, he has never abandoned the artistic and industrial arenas. While teaching in Vienna, he designed skis for Rossignol, made costumes for Sarah Jessica Parker in *Sex and the City* and for young British and American pop stars, and wrote songs for his wife, Mareva Galanter. His sixth sense intact, he has his finger on the pulse and possesses an undeniable talent for communicating that he combines with a delicate irony.

His style

Resolutely humorous. A long-time fan of the rectangle as a starting point, he dresses the female body in arty coats and concept tunics. Graffiti, geometric shapes, high-tech fabrics—carrying off his clothes has not always been easy. On the other hand, the "sandwich-women" know they are parading in a work of art, or in a product of the maestro's own unbridled imagination. Since 2000, he has reverted to more human proportions, and a joyous, zestful, feminine, more seductive style. Castelbajac catches trends on the wing: science fiction, regression, ecology, sex appeal, art, comics, and chews them up and spits them out in blousons, natty trapezoid dresses (carrying the flag for Courrèges), or helmets that he stages in playful shows not afraid to take a stand. His Obama dress has been much applauded, as has his Lowcost Luxury collection that promotes design at an accessible price. There was laughter when Sacha Baron Cohen reprised his role as Brüno down one of his catwalks, while it's not unknown to hit the dancefloor when live music blares out at his shows (for example by a group that translates as "Françoise's Thin Body").

Moreover, one has to concede that, thanks to his erudition and immense experience, the collections of Castelbajac—born in 1949, remember—remain ultramodern. His artistic instincts honed, he knows how to place graphics and illustrations on the body. His fashion, thanks to a variety of materials (from plastic to leather or cashmere) and simple cuts (from sheath dress to biker jacket, from bubble and puff dresses to T-shirts and skater skirts), conveys messages that hit home.

"All my inspiration has always come from my childhood."

MICHÈLE AND OLIVIER CHATENET, E2

Who are they?

They are a couple who grew up and flourished in the rag trade. They met when each was working as assistant to a designer: Thierry Mugler for Olivier and Rei Kawakubo (Comme des Garçons) for Michèle Meunier. This was in the 1980s, when the world of fashion was divided into two opposing camps: female warriors in stiletto heels, strapped into insolently curved suits (Mugler, Montana, Alaïa); and arty-cum-grunge, swathed in luxury rags, hovering between minimalism, deconstruction, and recherché graphics (the Japanese). Coming from opposite sides, they fell in love.

Married, they pooled their talents and launched a first experiment in 1987, under the name Mariot Chanet. The company went bankrupt, but the couple's talents were recognized and they were hired by Hermès. In 1999, they tried again with E2, centered on recycled materials and one-of-a-kind pieces. In 2001, the house of Leonard (founded 1958) turned to them to renew its collections. Finally, in 2005–10, stars like Madonna and Gwyneth Paltrow understood the benefit to be derived from turning out on the red carpet wearing a one-of-a-kind dress. The couple launched a diffusion line, Toiles et Reproductions, which reproduces the same model in nineteen copies, but in different fabrics.

Their style

Laden with history, with snippets of lives past. Be it a Chanel dress, or a Dior, Chloé, Laroche, Valentino, or Ralph Lauren, or a vintage 1950s, 1960s, or 1980s jacket snapped up in a market, or even a snatch of old Hermès silk, the important thing is the charm, the character exuded by a garment or a fabric. Tirelessly, they hunt down pieces of great value and make the most out of their designer heritage. Dab hands with scissors and needle, they unpick, recut, and rebuild. Everything is done by hand, and is, obviously, unique. A long evening dress can be repurposed as daywear. Less extravagantly, they might add braid to a sleeve or as an ornament or ribbon round the neckline, or morph a simple belt into a bejeweled marvel and embroider a dress. Often, they'll edge a hem, sleeve, or belt with little eyelets, swap buttons, or modernize by fraying or by refashioning the sleeves. If one had to define their hallmark, it would be an attraction for retro silks and vintage prints. They love embroidery, lace, and the couture, handmade touch. Not forgetting eyelets, their industrial signature. By infusing these collector's items with imaginative romanticism, they endow them with new life, a new way of being worn. And, at the same time, they are militants for luxury—very luxury—recycling. But, as all must acknowledge, history, revived by hand, has no price.

"Just as the new can appear outdated, the old can appear novel."

REI KAWAKUBO, COMME DES GARÇONS

Who is she?

The most austere, the least publicity-hungry, but also the most prosperous, of all Japanese designers. Designing clothing was not her objective, when, in 1964, she graduated in aesthetics and philosophy from Keio University, Tokyo. She initially worked as a photo stylist. Then, in despair at ever finding apparel corresponding to her taste, she decided to make clothes herself. This was in 1973, when she was thirty years old. Kawakubo christened her women's wear line with the unlikely name of Comme des Garçons.

In 1975, she presented her debut collection in Tokyo; three years later, she launched Comme des Garçons Homme, followed in 1981 by Comme des Garçons Tricot and Comme des Garçons Robe de Chambre. In 1981, she showed in Paris. An earthquake. Slap bang in the middle of upbeat, zestful "young designers"—all revisited fantasy and glamour—her collection certainly stood out: blacks, gray, white, ecru, asymmetric, perforated, frayed, off-kilter buttons, a sleeve missing or de trop—in short, guaranteed to cause a stir. Some went into raptures, others called it "Hiroshima chic," and worse. However, her company has continued to expand, and today produces some dozen lines. Earning plaudits from stars and intellectuals alike, delighted to be in fashion without appearing so, the look has an intriguing artiness that pushes comprehension to the limits. Among her early fans were Andy Warhol and Isabelle Adjani. To communicate her vision, the photo stylist in her publishes collections in splendid catalogs that bathe in her imaginative world, veritable works of art leaving her stamp on the company, the boutiques—in short, by the whole Comme des Garçons experience. In 1986, the

Pompidou Center selected some of her creations for the exhibition, *Mode et Photo*, while her influence on younger designers (Belgian, especially) was already palpable. She treats her celebrity cavalierly: no snob, she has collaborated with Nike, Lacoste, Converse, and, especially, H&M, but she also continues to be hands-on with innumerable collections coming out of the Aoyama studio in Tokyo. Very much concerned with store architecture, she will sometimes make room for other designers, as in her gigantic Dover Street Market in London. In 2004, she unleashed on the world's cities a string of temporary outlets that trade for just a year, calling them Guerrilla.

Her style

Radical, cerebral, rejecting all idea of seduction, based on natural materials with visible weave, less concerned with color (it's "distracting"), her style questions the notion of the beautiful, of the conventional in an attempt to reveal the personality of the wearer rather than encasing them in a definable look. The unfinished appearance of her (expensive) pieces speaks of a world in transformation, of transitory life, of a quest for essence.

Verging on the androgynous and melancholic, her collections speak of rigor and a rejection of all coquetry. Since the 1990s, her style has softened, and gained in color and femininity. Remaining timeless, it is rooted in materials and construction. She likes to reshape the anatomy, fashioning strange relief effects that distort the figure as if openly deriding the diktats of the perfect body. Playing with the various divisions of a garment, gloves, ribbons, trim, sleeves, or collar are applied in an incongruous, unexpected, humorous manner. In her winter 2007–08 show, for example, she pinned children's dresses onto the bust, combining them harmoniously and creating an authentic new garment. If she deliberately cultivates strangeness in willful opposition to the facile, her creations also enjoy a mysterious balance. The same equilibrium is at work between economic necessity and her intransigent creativity: though she might sell bags and accessories, her models parade without jewels or bags, sometimes without shoes. She may be pure, but she's not a purist.

"I don't have the impression of approaching fashion intellectually. I just want every piece I work on to be strong and beautiful."

ANN DEMEULEMEESTER

Who is she?

She is one of the "Antwerp Six" who were destined to sig-
nal a changing of the guard in European fashion (among
them, Dries Van Noten). A graduate—like her fellows—from
the prestigious Royal Academy of Fine Arts in Antwerp,
she won the prize for the most promising designer of the
year. This was in 1981, when she was twenty-two and
had no more money than any other graduate in her year.
Together, the six decided to rent a truck and present their
graduation collections in London. The British capital thus
discovered a younger generation that came from a country hitherto invisible on the fashion radar. As their names
seemed unpronounceable, columnists simply dubbed them
the "Antwerp Six." This did not sit well with them, however,
as each asserted their own personality.

In 1987, with her husband, photographer Patrick Robyn,
Ann founded her own house, BVBA 32. Three years later,
she showed in Paris with immediate success. Some even
enthusiastically hailed her as the "new Armani" because
of her timeless style. Today, this reserved woman with a
deep voice and slow output stands at the head of a very
prosperous company covering women's and men's lines,
jewelry, and accessories that makes thirty-five percent of
its turnover in the United States.

Her style

Her lines tend to the androgynous (she has produced
shows at which girls and boys descend the runway
together), narrow and black, all fine layers, lightly crumpled. Inspired by the music of Patti Smith, a friend from
way back, Ann Demeulemeester adores black and white;
or rather blacks and whites that vary according to the
structure of elaborately worked materials: large, loose knit,
gossamer-light sweaters, gleaming cigarette jeans in light
Lurex, biker jackets in distressed leather, meticulously finished light cashmere T-shirts. No ostentation. Everything's
in the detail: an edge with ribbon holes round a neckline,
discreetly laced sleeves, decreasing rows in knitwear, bias
cuts, jackets of classic appearance but with unexpected,
precise cuts.

Non-conformist, relatively indifferent to current trends,
she designs long dresses with romantic trains, poplin shirts
with unusual tails, vests to be worn open, punctuated with
rubbed aged metal jewelry and rocker boots, but together
the effect is romantic, sweetly poetic.

"Black is a family, a vocabulary; a black that doesn't have anything to say is a dead black."

ALBER ELBAZ

Who is he?

They say he possesses an innate feeling for female psychology. Can this have come from his two sisters? (He also has two brothers.) Or from memories of Casablanca, where he was born in 1961? Or, more simply, a modesty that gives him a wonderful ability to listen? Aged ten, his family emigrated to Israel, and he grew up in Holon, going on to study at Shenkar College of Engineering and Design at Ramat Gan, near Tel Aviv. He cut his teeth in New York, initially with a maker of formal gowns, then with Geoffrey Beene, where he learned a great deal, starting with an indifference to trends—and the art of draping, balance, and fall. Ten years later, he went to Paris and succeeded, in just one year at Guy Laroche, in reviving the style of the house. Pierre Bergé took him on at Saint Laurent's prêt-à-porter when Yves decided to devote his time solely to haute couture. Elbaz produced three much vaunted collections and would undoubtedly have succeeded to the couturier had the label not been bought out by the PPR Group, which parachuted in the redoubtable Tom Ford, the man behind the success of Gucci. Wanting to reign alone, Ford showed him the door. After a short stint with Krizia in Italy, Elbaz was called in by the new owners of Lanvin, where since 2001 he has performed wonders. Long considered a journeyman, someone to call on when things get tough, at Lanvin, he seems to be enjoying greener pastures.

His style

The years in the United States left him with excellent business savvy—a kind of courtesy, perhaps—that means that the customer's desires and morphology outweigh his own fantasies. On his arrival at Lanvin (a house founded by Jeanne Lanvin in 1909 and the oldest one still active), he dived into the inexhaustible storehouse of its archives, emerging with a wealth of inspiration: a mix of feminine chic and timeless elegance that he adapted over the years. His fabrics are natural, precious, and in general, plain: reams of silk, satin, ottoman, and taffeta. Sheath dresses of great distinction, easy to wear: classic or embellished with precious stones, refined accessories; asymmetric, with a gather down shoulder or hip. His shapely skirts follow a woman's curves to perfection, while the proportions of his jackets—waisted, belted—are impeccable. Preferring flat pleats to decorative overload, the keynote is harmony. He'll mix shiny and matt blacks, shades of red, burgundy, or airforce blue that can be livened up with a surprising splash of fuchsia or deep blue. His apparel simply never goes out of date. Whatever the season, his collections evince a charm, a grace, of which he is a master. Moreover, movie stars in Paris, New York, and Los Angeles have taken him to heart: There's hardly a red carpet without a complement of Lanvin dresses.

"I am not really a creative director. I don't like directing, I want to do things. And that takes time."

ALBERTA FERRETTI

Moreover, already the owner of the splendid Palazzo Donizetti in Milan (her showroom) she has also entirely restored a medieval village, Montegridolfo, whose castle has been turned into a luxury hotel, the Palazzo Viviani. In short, the cast-iron hand of industry in a velvet glove.

Who is she?

With a dressmaker mother, she grew up in the clothes trade. It was natural enough that, aged eighteen, in 1968, she would open her own shop at Cattolica, her native village on the shores of the Adriatic. She started out by selling the clothes of others, almost unknown at the time—Armani, Versace, Maruccia Mandelli—before hanging a few of her own designs on the racks. Her true debut collection dates to 1973. Since then, Ferretti has been slowly rising through the ranks, an understated ascendency, like her clothing. From the age of twenty-five she had to manage an increasingly sizable workshop, stores, orders, not to mention two young sons. But Italian fashion was making spectacular inroads abroad: with simple, feminine cuts, impeccable materials and finishing, it was easier to carry off than its French counterpart. In 1976, together with her brother, she launched AEFFE, a company that was to gradually make clothing for other designers, begining with Enrico Coveri. Its Italian expertise performed miracles: about fifteen years later, AEFFE was also manufacturing for Narciso Rodriguez, Jean Paul Gaultier, Rifat Ozbek, and Moschino. One of her sons is at the helm, in time-honored Italian tradition. As for her personal label, it has won over customers all around the world, a success from America to Japan, via Russia, Saudi Arabia, and Taiwan. Showbiz has not remained indifferent and her delicate chiffon dresses are regularly spotted on the red carpet on the likes of Nicole Kidman, Andie McDowell, Julia Roberts, and Uma Thurman.

The main collection has been joined by the less costly Philosophy di Alberta Ferretti line. With an acute talent for keeping ahead of the pack, her firm bought the leather company Pollini, extending its range to include accessories, lingerie, swimwear, children's wear, and fragrance.

Her style

Her clothes resemble their creator: fluid, diaphanous, laid-back, but with an unerring sense of detail. Much silk chiffon, plain, sometimes bright colors, drapery, judicious pleats, no overload, bias cut or Empire with ribbon bows—her wardrobe is one of Mediterranean elegance and sensuality. Less cluttered and more linear than bohemian chic, she cultivates a romantic side. Ferretti often projects her own image onto her models: determined to emphasize the female body, the clothes caress the curves without going overboard. She works with transparency, likes fine or layered straps, soft and fluid materials, but chic and intelligently cut. A real Italian, she takes great care over her knitwear: her sweaters are wonders of classicism, fine and ageless. Her combinations rely on contrasts between glossy and matt materials or between sleek and structured, sheer and dense. Overlays mix colors, in harmonious, unexpected duets. Whether for the Ferretti collection or second lines, Ferretti is past master at the art of proportion—neither too much nor too little, yet never tedious.

"My clothes aren't meant to be trendy at any cost. They are first and foremost an extension of the female personality."

JOHN GALLIANO

references to the homeless or the beauty of ugliness. "With each collection, I take on a role and really do base my work on history. It is part of to the creative process," he says. Moreover, at the end of each presentation, he takes to the runaway to accept the plaudits dressed—or disguised—in the spirit of his collection.

Who is he?

His runway shows are awaited as the weathervane to forthcoming trends. As creative director at Dior since 1997, this Englishman born in 1960 in Gibraltar has increased turnover fourfold in ten years. The product of multiculturalism and an overwhelming passion for fashion, he grew up flanked by two older sisters, Rosamaria and Immaculata, with a Spanish mother crazy about flamenco, and a father of Italian extraction, a plumber. He was just six when the family moved to south London, Battersea, still cosmopolitan and as yet ungentrified. This neighborhood of Indian, African, and Asian families was to be, as he said himself, "a formidable source of cultural enrichment," though his mother and sisters' taste for monastically immaculate white clothes did not always go unchallenged. After some years in a boys' school, John entered the famous Central Saint Martins College of Art and Design. At last in step with his passions, he worked like a Trojan, spending day and night in the library, while also working as a dresser at the theater. His baroque and extravagant graduation show entitled *French Revolution* was a huge hit. The clothes were shown in windows at Browns department store, but it proved a false start. Ruining himself with blockbuster collections, he was dropped by his financial backers. After ten years, in discouragement he moved to Paris, where Anna Wintour, editor in chief of *Vogue*, was determined to find him a sponsor (the Paine Webber banking group), and a venue for his shows (a manor owned by billionaire Sao Schlumberger). Takeoff at last! The scouts of Bernard Arnault, the owner of LVMH, spotted him and placed him with Givenchy for two years, but soon he was propelled to the top at Dior. He revived the slumbering firm with fairytale shows and sometimes uncomfortable themes, with

His style

Nothing is ever too much for John Galliano. Whether designing for his own house or for Dior, he runs through enormous bolts of fabric, which he often has printed, such as an eighteenth-century crinoline dress covered in newsprint. His Dior haute couture rustles to a shimmer of chiffon, velvet, and taffeta, reminiscent of the court of the Sun King, or rings to a profusion of pearls and raffia, as in his famous Masai collection. Some catwalk shows—veritable blockbusters—remain etched in the memory to this day: trapeze numbers, a vast mock souk, Shaolin monks above the runway, or flamenco-hip-hop-Bollywood crossovers. His models are coached like actresses. "I want agony in the expression and the clothes," he commands. "I want the models to look as if they've been dancing for eight days and eight nights." But he always keeps his feet on the ground. If his ready-to-wear sells like hot cakes, it's because he knows how to make his inspiration clear, to return to the sources of that Dior femininity, with constants such as small bust, narrow waist, sometimes with immense, puff sleeves, peplum jackets, 1950s skirt suits, glamorous sheath dresses, and a peccadillo for lingerie. Fascinated by the cuts of his go-to couturiers, Madeleine Vionnet, remembered for her bias cuts, and Azzedine Alaïa, he extrapolates his own, playing with modern transparencies, blazing colors, and flounces. His tottering shoes—the terror of his models—are the finishing touch for a silhouette like that of a sexy dragonfly, a dapper little marquis or duchess set off by invariably sophisticated makeup.

"Style is: wearing an evening dress to McDonald's, wearing heels to play football. It is personality, confidence and seduction."

JEAN PAUL GAULTIER

His style

He gave fashion a real social content and was able to sniff out trends and make them part of his work. He thus incorporated the dominating influence of English punk in the 1970s, which still today permeates his style: extravagant, "lost generation," uncompromisingly sexy. He imposes modern sex appeal on both genders. For Gaultier, women, like the men, assume their desires. She wears laced sheath dresses with cut panels, bust-enhancing corsets, subdued colors often enlivened with a bright line or a dazzling strap. She can be slightly edgy—very Parisian. As for the male of the species, he has something graceful, vulnerable about him, at odds with in-your-face gay eroticism: tight T-shirts, fishnets, tattoo style (that also features on the women). For men, Gaultier even embraces the skirt (starting, in 1985) and bright colors. He has a knack for extraordinary associations such as billowing tartan skirts (he adores the kilt) with an austere masculine jacket. Thanks to him, the leather biker jacket over a sheer chiffon dress became a left-field classic.

As for models, he has never reneged on his origins and childlike curiosity: he prefers "characters" over traditional good looks. The plump, the colorful, the streetwise, and seniors alike are welcome at his runway shows. The construction of his apparel is worth observing: classic couture with contemporary details—original stripes or intriguing slits. A Gaultier jacket lasts forever.

Who is he?

The archetypal extravert French eccentric. He was one of a throng of "young designers" who turned the accepted norms of beauty on their head in 1980s. The only child of an accountant and a cashier, he grew up in Arcueil in the Paris suburbs. He would watch his grandmother reading cards for her neighbors; at a very young age she also taught him how to sew. But he felt the hand of destiny one day at the movies when they were showing *Paris Frills*, made by Jacques Becker in 1944. A poor student at school, he was crazy about fashion drawing. By fifteen he was sketching entire collections inspired by fashion magazines that he would mail to Pierre Cardin, among others. In 1970, Cardin hired him. Jean Paul was eighteen.

Working with Jacques Esterel, Jean Patou, and then back with Cardin, in 1976, his debut collection was a flop. Deflated, he was thinking of throwing in the towel when the Japanese group Kashiyama, a manufacturer and distributor of ready-to-wear, threw him a lifeline. The 1980s saw his eventual triumph: accessories, men's lines, fragrances, and even furniture. He designed costumes for a ballet by Régine Chopinot and—in 2009—by Angelin Preljocaj, for concerts by Madonna and Mylène Farmer. He co-presented a TV show with Antoine de Caunes, *Eurotrash*, and did costumes for the cinema: *Kika* by Pedro Almodovar, Luc Besson's *The Fifth Element*, and *The City of Lost Children* by Jeunet and Caro. From 2004 to 2010, Hermès commissioned him to create its ready-to-wear and took up a solid position in his firm. He is the only designer today to successfully juggle haute couture and prêt-à-porter.

"It was by listening to my grandmother advising her customers that I learned how women think, about their relationship with beauty."

MARITHÉ + FRANÇOIS GIRBAUD

Who are they?

They are the high priests of denim who have been experimenting tirelessly for forty years: stonewash (which they invented), resin-coatings, laser cut, and heat-bonded (without sewing). François, born in Mazamet in southern France in 1942, has a working-class background and has kept a strong humanist touch as well as a slightly anarchic spirit.

When in the 1960s he met Marithé, his future wife, from Lyon, they opened a shop and imported American jeans that they restyled, rechristening them Goulue, or Pépère. French teenyboppers lapped them up. In 1982, they set up their own label. As the jeans market began to nosedive, their main European distributor folded in 1991. But there was no stopping them. Today, they are very ecologically committed: since 2003, to roll back the polluting effects of washing and limit water consumption, they have been developing a 97.5 percent waterfree treatment, WattWash. Then came their Reversible brand bags in recycled PVC. Lastly, with Ingeo, they launched a line of biodegradable clothes in corn fiber with a smaller carbon footprint than petrochemical textiles and are one hundred percent renewable.

The brand scandalized Catholics in 2005 with an ad campaign replacing the apostles in Leonardo da Vinci's *Last Supper* with women. They won the ensuing lawsuit, hugely boosting their profile in the process. Now over sixty years old, they say they're still indifferent to the vagaries of fashion, but always on the hunt for lifestyle ideas. In fact a positive Girbaud "tribe" has grown up.

Their style

Jeans in their luxury, design incarnation. Their prices are as high as in the most upmarket boutique. One pops into Girbaud as one would into a workshop, to get a flavor of new interpretations of street fashion. The baggy cut, in a multitude of guises, remains a point of reference, along with a white shirt, but these two classics are put through their style paces: asymmetric and laced, pleats, shirrs, slits, rips, or button-up inserts—they play with hip, waist, and shoulder placement. There are also urban lines—smarter, and more classically elegant, but still with that dash of arty inventiveness: T-shirts soberly underscored by graphic patterns, elaborately cut and intriguing openings in the jeans, pants with creases (as with dresses and jackets), complicated decorative stitching, glossy coatings, wide jackets and coats loosely secured with ties. Decreasing stitches on ultrafine knitwear jerseys makes them hug the bust. Denser knits (a touch ethnic) gracefully float up or bunch. The fallback colors remain blue—a splendid range, from deep purple through their "true blue" to skyblue—gray in all shades, white, and black.

"The history of the blue jean follows that of society. We are the designers designing jeans 'live.'"

RICCARDO TISCI FOR GIVENCHY

Who is he?

In 2005, at the age of thirty, he took on the daunting task of succeeding Alexander McQueen and John Galliano as creative director at Givenchy. An Italian from the south, born into a family of eight girls in the village of Tarente, he started working aged just sixteen in a bid for independence. He left the nest at seventeen, heading for London, despite not speaking a word of English. Awarded a scholarship, he entered Central Saint Martins College of Art and Design with the intention of studying art, in the end opting for fashion. After graduating in 1999, he netted jobs freelancing for several brands, including Puma, Coccapani, and Ruffo Research. In 2004, he presented a collection of his own in Milan. At this time the LVMH group proposed that he replace Julien McDonald (who succeeded McQueen) at Givenchy. His debut show was tepidly received by journalists, more accustomed to the extravagances of his predecessors. But quietly, methodically, Tisci has begun to impose his romantic and sensual vision. In 2008, Madonna commissioned a series of costumes. That same year, he was handed the direction of the house's image and menswear lines.

His style

Unlike Alber Elbaz for Lanvin or Lagerfeld at Chanel, Riccardo Tisci does not try to follow in the footsteps of the founder of the house, Hubert de Givenchy, or even to revisit the classics worn by Audrey Hepburn. To impose his ideas against the backdrop of strong personalities such as Galliano and McQueen, who produced some clamorous collections in the house before him, the young Italian places his trust in updated romanticism. He likes white, black, muted tones, and fluid lines, and can design a loose trouser suit as well as a skirt billowing with feathers or pleats topped by a soberly buttoned blouse. His dresses are based on classic lines, but with atypical, asymmetric openings and a pattern of ties on the back. The description of Gothic has been suggested, but actually his style is far softer, featuring a natural melancholy. The women he dresses are sensitive to underplayed elegance, never provocative, and place more store by their likes and dislikes than by modishness. Two of his fans give a good idea of the style: Queen Rania of Jordan and the actress Cate Blanchett.

"The world of fashion is contaminated by information, trends, and stars. Let's stay pure, in tune with our real desires."

ANNE VALÉRIE HASH

Who is she?

She is a pure product of French know-how, who sells far more abroad than in her own country. Indeed 95 percent of her sales turnover derives from export. Born in Paris and with a CV that includes the Duperré Higher School of the Applied Arts, a Parisian dressmaking school run by the Chambre Syndicale, and Temple University, Philadelphia, where she studied art and drawing, she returned to her native city for some hands-on experience: with Dior, Chanel, Lacroix, Ricci, and Hubert Barrère, a specialist in corsetry.

In 2000, aged twenty-nine, she produced her first runway show, which was greeted with enthusiasm by the press. Since then she has designed many collections and been invited several times to feature on haute couture catwalks, while simultaneously designing models for Monoprix that partly enable her to finance her own label. In 2005, she received support from an investment fund, Mode et Finance (set up by Didier Grumbach, president of the Fédération Française de la Couture) intended for young designers. In 2009, she designed for the 3 Suisses mail-order company. And, as a young mom with two girls, she has launched Mademoiselle, a collection for children. In 2011, she plans to brings out an accessibly priced diffusion line. Her clients include Naomi Watts, Uma Thurman, Cate Blanchett, and Vanessa Paradis.

Her style

Anne Valérie Hash started out putting a twist on men's clothing, but now she is increasingly taking a more resolutely feminine and gentle approach. Fluid lines, skimming but not molding the body, washed colors that clad, caress, and emphasize the figure. Her dressmaking experience shows through in perfect construction and cut, in handmade finishings and details, and in combinations of materials.

With her dressmaking workshop situated a stone's-throw away from the design studio, she tries her hand at pieces verging almost on haute couture: a dress built in a fan shape with a hundred seams, hand-frayed tulle for a fur effect, translucent dyes—a diluted rainbow on a sheath dress.

She has explored high-tech fabrics—metallic or iridescent (and extremely expensive)—made by the Swiss manufacturer Jakob Schlaepfer. Her drapery is redolent of Ancient Greece. She has, however, not entirely abandoned the masculine style that she now tones down and refines: single-breasted jackets, overcoats, and straight-legged pants add a more severe touch to the otherwise curvy lines.

"Couture is a different kind of emotion. It will not die because men have hands to work with and these hands will always want to express themselves through craftsmanship."

MARC JACOBS

Who is he?

He has often stated that his vocation as a designer originated with his grandmother—"the most important person in my life." Born into a well-off New York family in 1963, he lost his father at age seven. Traipsing, with his brother, through his mother's three subsequent marriages, he decided at sixteen to move in with "grandma." She offered him stability and taught him to knit and show. He discovered fashion while still at high school during an odd job he took with Charivari, a trendy boutique of neo-hippie inclinations. On advice from the designer Perry Ellis, he enrolled at Parsons School for Design. After studying for four years, his finals' project made quite an impact: a collection of handmade oversize sweaters decorated with bright pink smileys. In the showroom, the buyer Robert Duffy was enthusiastic and proposed a joint venture but, for want of funds, the concern never saw the light of day. In 1984 Perry Ellis recruited both—Marc for creation, Duffy for management—before dying of AIDS in 1986. In 1992, the firm asked Marc Jacobs to take over the reins. Alas, the grunge inspiration of the thirty-year-old designer clearly marked by intimations of mortality scandalized a company more at home with sport chic. The duo was given the pink slip, but in 1994 managed to float their own label. The success was at once critical and commercial, columnists and buyers alike applauding a collection for which supermodel friends like Linda Evangelista and Naomi Campbell, among others, performed the honors.

In 1997, the LVMH group turned to him for a whole new prêt-à-porter collection for Louis Vuitton. A triumph. Following this, Marc Jacobs supervised Vuitton's entire production portfolio, from clothing to accessories to windows and ads. With a fair proportion of the revenues being swallowed up by a burgeoning art collection, a profitable collaboration arose between Vuitton and artists such as Sprouse, Murakami, and Prince. Firmly ensconced in the LVMH group, his label thrives and multiplies its market niches: diffusion lines, children's wear and menswear, fragrance, and accessories. With friends in showbiz and his lovers, Jacobs is a party animal with a high profile, as witnessed by the close-ups of his many tattoos, but he has also suffered from a serious drug and alcohol addiction problem that he tackled in 2007. Now less wild, he campaigns for humanitarian causes and on public health issues.

His style

Unlike certain designers, it's hard to speak of a style immediately recognizable through some specific trait. Once the king of grunge, Marc Jacobs still has his finger on the pulse. Far from ever claiming to invent, he glories in his references, in particular the 1970s—to the point of running into trouble with a Swedish designer from those years who accused him of ripping off one of his prints for a scarf. The affair was resolved with dollars. Jacobs succeeds in mixing and stylizing various eras into an entirely contemporary cocktail, a hotchpotch of girly, punk, or hippie (depending on the years), and chic. In his most expensive collection, he is capable of elaborate pieces of complex construction worthy of Japanese designers, as well as some irresistibly fashionable and easy-to-wear apparel for his diffusion lines. 1950s or 1980s references can be picked up here and there, but they are always presented with an indefinable post-millennium twist—the length of sleeves or trousers, the width of a lapel, the refinemant of a belt, some retro stripes, muted and gaudy colors, or punchy prints. All together the effect is irresistible.

"It doesn't really matter what the trend is or what the look is. You've got to have one. So I find it's like a cartoon world out there where everyone's sort of playing dress-up, and that's why I say there are no bad trends."

RABIH KAYROUZ

Who is he?

An insanely talented Lebanese of inexhaustible enthusiasm. Born in 1973, a graduate of the dressmaking arm of the Paris Chambre Syndicale in 1992, he cut his teeth with Dior and Chanel before returning to Lebanon. At the time, between 1995 and 2000, the country was enjoying a rebirth and many Lebanese intellectuals were returning after the civil war. Feeling the same buzz, Rabih established a little workshop to carry out an order for a wedding dress.

Consequently, his career took off thanks to orders from elegant customers and word of mouth. In parallel, he worked for a women's magazine, designing a dress that made the cover and earned several orders.

He is young, and belongs neither to the world of couture nor to that of more famous dressmakers—such as Elie Saab—whose sumptuous wedding dresses and evening gowns are encrusted with gems and aimed at well-heeled Middle Eastern customers. His inventiveness and meticulous technique, allied to a great ability to listen, have made him a roaring success. (He has produced some 300 wedding dresses.) He set up his house in 2003, staging a show in Beirut in 2004. But the assassination of Prime Minister Hariri and of Gebran Tueni the following year, followed by the war in 2006, brought a halt to proceedings. He continues to trade, but no longer puts on runway shows. In 2008, anxious to promote young Lebanese designers and helped by a friend, he opened a boutique-laboratory, Starch, in the center of Beirut where four to six talented young fashion graduates selected by jury receive guidance and present their work. In 2009, he opened a showroom in Paris in the former Théâtre de Babylone on boulevard Raspail, and, invited by the Chambre Syndicale de la Couture Parisienne, he presented his designs in its official calendar. His creativity appears intact, and he's lost none of his enthusiasm, but he doesn't want to leave Beirut "where people *really* love dressing."

His style

All delicacy, femininity, and clarity, Kayrouz's clothes hardly touch the body. Be it silk, silk gazar, or organza, wool or fine cashmere, the cuts follow the curves like a cloud. Skillful placement makes a plunging back stand out slightly from the skin, sweeping down to create a feel of relaxed sensuality. He likes to see how the light falls on and through a garment. Neckline, sleeves, and hems are underlined by a plethora of hand finishing. Feathers appiled one by one enliven a blouse, the curve of a shoulder. Fine saddle-stitched vertical flounces curve the back, recalling the Dior or Cardin of the 1950s. His knitted dresses, ribbed, fluttering on the hips, make one think of Alaïa, the whole giving an impression of unostentatious opulence, of extreme quality. There's no room for loud prints in this carefully studied modernity. Couture technique and experimentation with fabric underpin each collection.

"When I'm designing, I don't only look at a woman's body, I look at how she wears her clothes."

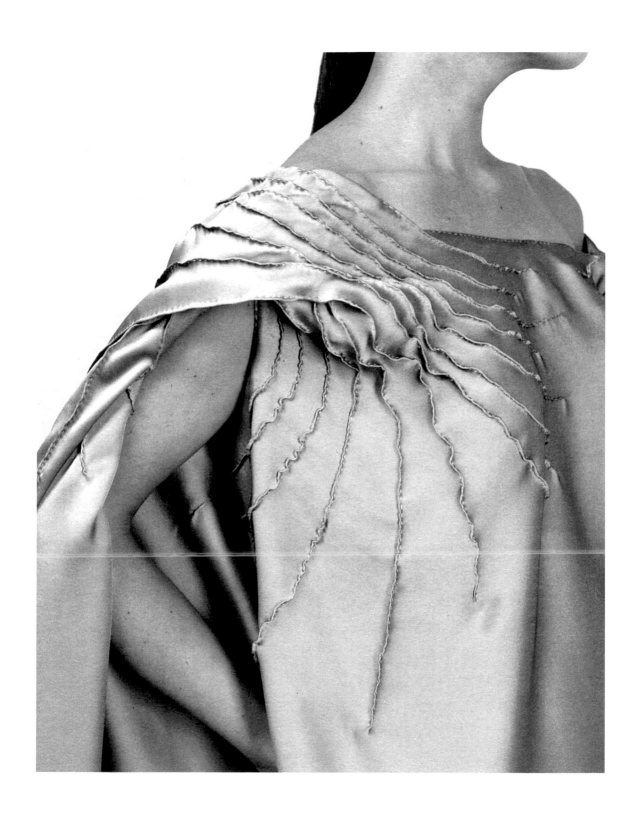

JEAN-PAUL KNOTT

Who is he?

A Belgian who grew up in New York and absorbed the fundamentals of the trade at the Fashion Institute of Technology. Gifted and passionate, he obtained his diploma in two years instead of four. After an internship with Krizia in New York, he went to Paris, and joined Yves Saint Laurent as a trainee, climbing the ladder in thirteen fertile years: he became assistant, then in 1996, designer for the Saint Laurent Rive Gauche line. Yves Saint Laurent bowed out of prêt-à-porter in 1999, coinciding with the arrival of Tom Ford (the firm had just been bought out by the PPR Group).

Making way to the American, Knott decided to create his own label. Presented in Paris, Brussels, and New York in 2000, his first women's collection was much applauded. At the same time, Knott took up a post as creative director at Krizia—an old acquaintance—then Louis Féraud, streamlining and modernizing collections. He designed costumes for a ballet by Béjart, as well as a collection for Dim, and even decorated a room for Royal Windsor in Brussels. From 2007 to 2009, he served as head of women's wear at Cerruti. In Brussels, he set up a store-gallery to exhibit a selection of artists. Along the way he has also designed some pieces for the 3 Suisses mail-order catalog and, together with a Japanese businessman, developed a line of more accessible, machine-washable clothing sold not out of the Knott Galerie, but at other points of sale.

His style

Characterized by explorations of the theme of sobriety. With a rectangle of fabric, he can create ten different volumes. Or fit a bias-cut dress by rolling it around the body like a toga. He has thought long and hard about drape, investing it with modernity and dynamism, and works on primary colors, abstract patterns, some hand-painted, on marked contrasts in material, on proportions.

Hired by the UN in the context of climate change awareness in December 2009 at the Copenhagen Summit, he launched an eco-conscious T-shirt one could design oneself. Moreover he believes in the future of "clothing as investment, timeless and comfortable."

"Clothing resembles more an applied than a pure art. It includes the art of business and longevity."

SOPHIA KOKOSALAKIS

Who is she?

For the general public, her name came to prominence at the Athens Olympics in 2004: she designed costumes for the 6,000 performers in the opening and closing ceremonies, as well as the eye-popping dress that encased Björk in a 900-yard stream of sky-blue chiffon. Born in the city in 1972, she took a first degree in literature there before coming to London to study for a diploma at the Central Saint Martins College of Art and Design.

In 1999, she launched her own label at the same time as designing for the Italian brand, Ruffo Research. Then, in 2006, she was sought out by the house of Madeleine Vionnet to revive a house that had been dormant for forty years. She resigned two years later, apparently to be able to devote her time fully to her label, although it is rumored that is was because the manual labor involved in her sublime gowns made them simply too expensive to execute. In 2009, came the volte-face: Diesel commissioned her to design for their Black Gold collection. Not one to be put off by a challenge, she also agreed to design a mini collection for Top Shop. "Fashion is made to be worn, if not, it's a flop," she insists. So there you go.

Her style

Sophia is Greek and if, at the beginning, she distanced herself from the culture of her homeland, she has returned to draw on a superb vein of inspiration, surely also inspired by the Vionnet archives. Her silk drapery revisits classicism: all in lightness, her dresses feature fine piping, puckered here and there as if by a wound, delicately ruffled, swelling like waves, arabesques sculpted out of fabric. She plays the femininity card with bustiers chiseled with motifs in relief in a smoky hue, black, or ivory. Horizontal drape straps in the bust or flows from the waist, unhampered, awash with volutes. Or the whole body is draped, like a retro evening gown, but modernized with lines of topstitching.

If she harbors a soft spot for inlays, as well as for old gold, she is also fond of black, leather in particular, embellished with yokes that can verge on overkill, chiffon, or metallic embroidery. The work is as precise as couture.

"I always employ the same vocabulary, but over the years I have managed to compose more complicated, more original sentences with it. This has taken me a very long time."

KARL LAGERFELD

Who is he?

Initiates don't even use his surname anymore. He's simply Karl, as people would say Marilyn or Coco. Karl is, above all, a character. Cultured, polyglot (German, English, French, and Italian are among the seven languages he speaks), he's a collector of art, old books, and houses, adores architecture, does his own fashion photographs (in schematic black and white), owns a bookstore in Paris, a gallery, and a publishing house. He is, in his own words, "a professional dilettante." Exceptionally gifted, his upbringing was solitary, his nose always in books. In 1954, he carried off first prize (sharing it with Yves Saint Laurent) of the International Wool Secretariat organized by Woolmark with a sketch for a coat.

His parents had just moved from Hamburg to Paris where he loved to accompany his mother to haute couture fittings. He was hired immediately by Balmain, who made him his assistant for three and a half years. After a brief stint with Jean Patou, he went freelance, accumulating contracts in France, Italy, Germany, and Japan. He is the man behind the success of Chloé and Fendi furs. But it is, of course, with Chanel, beginning in 1983, that his designing talents have truly come into their own. He has modernized the house and, in an extraordinary tour de force, embodied its image in the person of Ines de la Fressange. He has had less success with his own labels, Karl Lagerfeld and K by Karl. Iron-willed, he also made a name for himself thanks to a metamorphosis in 2000: unable to get into slim-fitting suits by Hedi Slimane for Dior Homme, he shed ninety-three pounds in thirteen months. Slimane has since moved on, but Karl has kept his weight down.

His style

With a sixth sense for trends, his talent is to grasp the essence of a house. When, as at Chanel, he has the good fortune to be able to draw on a strong concept, he is capable of adopting and renewing it for more than twenty years. Today, the famous braid-trimmed jackets with patch pockets have become classics people cannot get enough of. He rings the changes: checked, torn, narrow, sequined, in raffia, in raw linen, or "Chinesed" (with a Mao collar). He adorns them with lengths of lace, anchors them with great motorcycle boots or clogs, and sprays them in sequins or chiffon.

With his nose for marketing and a dose of humor, he knows how to keep the faithful happy with the eternal little black dress, cascades of pearls, and the black-and-white silk blouse, as well as reeling in a younger set who fight for the 2.55 bag reinterpreted in straw, tweed, nylon, and even plastic. At Chanel, Karl has managed to marry grunge, Lolita, punk, graffiti, and sport; he's designed moon boots and even tattoos. Chanel, in the reign of Karl, has dressed three generations, but without forfeiting the Coco spirit, a sparkling, feminine insolence.

"**Fashion is an attitude more than a clothing detail.**"

ALEXANDER MCQUEEN

His style

A provocative genius. He possessed a staggering feel for volume—like his compatriot John Galliano (working for the rival LVMH group). McQueen was afraid of nothing, neither eighteenth-century references, nor extravagance, nor luxury, which he savaged with intelligence: felted cashmere, mohair lace sewn with precious stones, leather worked as tortoiseshell, shock-tactic combinations—metal, plastic, and feathers, all worked as couture.

His shows may have been dreamy or trashy, but always intensely powerful and the lines always recognizable. Cinched waists, magical curves—his mastery of bias cutting was second to none—bright prints, strange optical effects, sumptuous materials, very futuristic Grand Siècle, always with a concept behind it: recycling or the deep sea (he enjoyed diving). The man was a poet, a prolific designer, but one with a real political conscience.

Who is he?

This sensitive Englishman was long trailed as the bad boy of fashion. For example, his stint at Givenchy—from 1996 to 2001, just after Galliano—was scandalous: he lambasted his first collection as "crap" and, the following year, shocked columnists and buyers with a runway show during which robots squirted paint on to white dresses. He had moreover invited Aimee Mullins, a double amputee who took to the runway on carved wooden legs. Phew! Nevertheless, for this son of a cab driver born in East London, fashion was an abiding passion from a young age. He made dresses for his three sisters and left school at sixteen to train with the prestigious Anderson & Sheppard on Savile Row, then—among others—with costumiers Angels and Berman. He then crossed the Channel to work with Romeo Gigli in Milan. Rather late, in 1994 at twenty-five and with experience under his belt, he entered the famous Central Saint Martins College of Art and Design. His graduate collection was bought lock, stock, and barrel by the stylist Isabella Blow, who was to become a close friend (Blow would commit suicide in 2007). Björk commissioned an outfit from him for the cover of her album *Homogenic* in 1997. He could give free rein to his talents with his own label, founded in 2001 with the assistance of the PPR Group. Each of his runway shows was explosively inventive. The world of rock music for one was head over heels. Alas, in February 2010, he took his own life at his home.

"There is something sinister, something quite biographical about what I do. It's my personal business. I think there is a lot of romance, melancholy. There's a sadness to it, but there's romance in sadness. I suppose I am a very melancholy person."

DRIES VAN NOTEN

Who is he?

Born into a family of tailors, during the war his ingenious grandfather would turn old garments inside out and restyle them. Their first clothing store was in his home city of Antwerp. His mother ran a store selling fabric and old lace, while his father owned two vast outlets selling major menswear brands. The son accompanied his father to prêt-à-porter shows in Milan and Paris. In such an environment, the young Dries, born in 1958, decided he would become a designer rather than a salesman. During his studies at the Royal Academy of Fine Art in Antwerp, he was already working freelance for a Belgian manufacturer. In 1986, he launched out under his own name. His success was immediate in New York and London, as well as in Belgium. From the beginning he used the same fabrics for men and women. Today, with boutiques in world capitals, he remains self-financed.

His style

He is the lyric poet of color. Each runway show displays a virtuoso harmony of tones that at first sight seem incompatible. Neither complementary nor monochrome. In his sober pants-blouse-jacket, skirt-blazer, and coat-dress ensembles, Dries tends to the unconventional: old rose-iced chestnut-orange, or mustard-beige, eggplant-celadon. He revels in the contrast between the muted and the saturated. His instantly recognizable prints complete an impression of discord: abstract brushstrokes, stylized plants, patchwork. Here a motif of crumpled gray croc, there a flash of charcoal gray leopard, or foliage on a pearl ground. Over the course of his collections, he has wedded geometric forms such as squares, stripes, and dotted lines, and explored ethnic patterns. His garments never hug, but lightly float, falling perfectly. In such downplayed femininity, free of impertinent décolletés, the word "sexy" would sound obscene.

"My Belgian nationality is a source of pride, an integral part of my story. Paris can be a challenge ... or a safety net."

PHOEBE PHILO

Who is she?

One of the most talented and modest of contemporary designers. With Stella McCartney, she kick-started the label Chloé. It was in 1997: Karl Lagerfeld had left, and the house was drifting a little. It was rumored that by calling on the daughter of Paul McCartney for the position of creative director, Chloé was just out to hog the media limelight. McCartney quickly found her feet, however, calling in reinforcements from her friend Phoebe, a graduate, like her, of Central Saint Martins College in London. Together, they massively boosted sales. When Stella McCartney left Chloé to create her own line, Phoebe naturally replaced her as head designer with brilliant results. She added a pair of two mid-season collections to the two preexisting ones. The brand owes her one of its bestsellers: the Paddington handbag with its impressive brass padlock. Faced with an unruly queue in front of its London store, they had to call in the police to ensure the deliveries made it in safely. Sofia Coppola and Milla Jovovich are fans. Born in Paris in 1973 and educated in England, Phoebe Philo has earned a professional reputation as strong in marketing as in design, but also as a woman determined not to let her business activities ruin her private life. After the birth of her daughter (with the art dealer Max Wigram in 2005), in 2006 she decided to withdraw from the scene to devote more time to her family. Two years later she found herself back in the saddle when the LVMH group offered her the creative directorship at Céline, replacing Ivana Omazic. Realistic in a market that has to cater to its existing customer base, she has patiently built up a heritage, a kind of DNA code around which each collection revolves.

Her style

The word romantic is bandied about. Wrongly. She's far better than that. Phoebe Philo provides a soberly graphic reinterpretation of modernity. At both Chloé and Céline—brands evoking a vaguely 1970s femininity—she gently brought the past into clearer focus. She has developed an ultra-feminine silhouette, without yielding to froufrous or flash-in-the-pan trends: studied lines, dynamic, an adult sensuality, brought out by stiff materials, an understated palette. In keeping with her character, she loathes anything flashy. Result: though her style is quite recognizable, her garments are almost timeless. She does not go in for ostentatious demonstrations of talent. Plain colors, white, black, tobacco, and natural tones—a nod to an ecologist streak—no superfluous adornments, but balanced compositions, in pure lines, easy to wear. Elegance tinged with austerity, yet with ample room for leather, one of Céline's leading products.

"I try to be simple and authentic: beautiful clothing with meaning, emotion, and structure."

MIUCCIA PRADA

Who is she?

The most astonishing success on the whole fashion scene. Now over sixty, the mother of two boys, she is anything but frivolous. She intended to enter politics and indeed was an activist for the Italian Communist Party. While studying political science, she was a passionate theater lover, took lessons in mime, and worked for women's rights.

A year after her degree, in 1971, she went to work at Fratelli Prada, the company founded by her grandfather, Mario Prada, in 1913. The luggage company quietly catered for its Milanese customers with beautiful bags made to last, the logo discreetly engraved in the leather or the fabric. Miuccia designed—half-heartedly—the accessories. In 1978, she met her husband-to-be, Patrizio Bertelli, who owned a leather factory in Florence, and the spark was lit. She took over the company and they launched a debut collection of shoes. "She has the instinct, me, the analysis. Together, we arrive at the same place," says her husband. The house began to turn heads in 1985, with the famous nylon bags emblazoned with a triangular metal logo. An immediate triumph, the model was copied a thousand times. In 1989 came women's prêt-à-porter; in 1992, the appearance of a younger, fresh-faced, and less expensive line, Miu Miu. In 1994, they designed their first menswear collection, meeting with the same success. But it is thanks to Bertelli that Prada has become a luxury prêt-à-porter group, an empire: successively, he purchased slices of Fendi, Helmut Lang, Jil Sander, and Alaïa, only to offload them in 2005–7. Too onerous, too complicated, too expensive, too far removed from the handicraft where they started. They prefer to devote their time to the America's Cup, to which they contribute a boat each year, and to the foundation for contemporary art set up in 1995. The house inspired the title of a film, *The Devil Wears Prada*, as well as spawning an unauthorized biography in Italy, a behind-the-scenes bestseller that presented the couple as intransigent, whimsical, and quick to anger. But isn't that what all successful people are like?

Her style

The designer has little time for the press, but avowed one day that she creates "less for a woman's body, more for her brain." This is a good summary of the austere femininity of a style in which strange combinations and kitsch prints question the traditional idea of good taste. Prada likes rigid materials, sober cut, dark colors, and retro patterns. A silhouette of understated sex appeal that eschews blatant eroticism, yet revels in plunging V-necks, without jewels, or collars buttoned up to the throat. Ornamentation tends to be confined to the shoes: chunky but very high heels in contrasting colors or carved like a jewel. It was Miuccia Prada who launched bare legs, even with a dressy suit. Her clothes do not rely on hue-and-cry, but on surprising associations. Prada prefers modest straight skirts that can be boring, but also likes brightly colored pleated silks. Her work on lace avoids the pretty-pretty and finesse, using the material like wrough iron, imparting a dynamic modernity. Passionate about vintage clothes, she references them constantly in collections that sometimes evoke Anna Magnani, sometimes Hollywood of the 1940s and 1950s.

"My clothes are instant commentaries on what surrounds us; they are my way of reacting by means of fashion."

RODARTE

Who are they?

Kate and Laura Mulleavy, two sisters from California, who never went to fashion school, suddenly emerged into the world of fashion in New York in 2005. Born in Oakland in 1979 and 1981 respectively, with a mother with an artistic bent—she now designs jewels for Rodarte—and a botanist father, they spent their childhood exploring the forests of Muir in search for mushrooms and other plants that would end up under dad's microscope. When not running around outside, they'd watch horror films or observe stragglers of the punk or hippie movements in the streets of Capitola and then Pasadena, where the family moved in 1996. Kate studied Art History and Laura English Literature at Berkeley. Passionate about clothing, its function, its expressiveness, and its construction, they learned and developed their style by pulling apart pieces made by others (Chanel in particular), and analyzing them. Like a schismatic religion, their collections have an aura of a mysticism to which New York department store buyers seem receptive. They announced their arrival in Manhattan by dispatching, not the traditional catalog with a debut collection, but a swarm of little paper dolls reproducing their Rodarte creations (from the maiden name of their mother who offered them such encouragement). From *Vogue* to Bergdorf Goodman and *Women's Wear Daily*, everyone went mad for them. In three years, they conquered the arbiters of fashion and showbiz (Cate Blanchett, Keira Knightley), carried off awards and, even better, one of their ensembles was promptly snapped up by none other than the Costume Institute.

Tireless workers, obsessed by experimentation with fabrics and prints, they have been hired by Gap and Target to design capsule collections.

Their style

Romanticism and melancholy, with a flutter of sublimated grunge. Some of their dresses give the impression of luxurious ragbags—scraps of chiffon thrown on as if haphazardly. In fact, the Mulleavy sisters painstakingly devise wearable outfits perfectly adapted to the body. Their inspiration is fed by folk tales or the movies, ghosts of ancestral tribes or impoverished women from Santa Cruz. Silk, lace, leather, chiffon dyed and re-dyed, twists, knots, macramé, crochet, tattoo prints—allusions to craftsmanship and long-lost epochs blend together, revisited in an avant-garde cocktail. Their collections emanate a languor, a delicacy, unfolding against a backdrop of creative intransigence in a honey-sweet ambience of a phantasmagorical road movie. Gothic ramblings—at any moment one expects a shaman to turn up.

"We didn't have formal training. That is kind of indicative of an American: a naïve quality and at the same time a fierce determination."

SONIA AND NATHALIE RYKIEL

Who are they?

By the 1960s, Sonia Rykiel was being hailed as the queen of knitwear as, before anyone else, she had understood the potential of wool and breathed new life into the twin-set. By 1968, her sweaters and knit dresses sold out of her store in Saint-Germain-des-Prés were doing *very* nicely. Bang in the middle of the protest movement, she put out clothing with visible stitching that also upset bourgeois sensibilities. Her red hair is as well known as her label, while her taste for literature makes her an emblematic Left Bank personality (the family has a table reserved for them for lunch at the Café de Flore). Her daughter Nathalie, who was a krack for marketing, took over in the 2000s: widening the range, she focuses on a younger market (Inscription Rykiel) for children, launches three fragrances, and made ripples in 2002 with a line of sex toys elegantly packaged in black and pink satin. It was a commercial and media success. Systematically and unflinchingly—and inspired by her three daughters—she rejuvenated the customer base. Her two capsule collections for H&M in 2009 and 2010 were snapped up in twenty-four hours, confirming the vitality of the label.

Their style

The dilemma with a label strongly marked by its creator is how to keep it going. For more than forty years, Sonia Rykiel (born in 1930) made her own designs for striped body-hugging knitwear, skirts with suspenders, tight sweaters with scoop necklines (sometimes with amusing or puzzling slogans inscribed in rhinestone on black), cropped wrap tops or long and belted ones, thick, brightly colored fur coats, and for evening, the legendary plunging V-neckline gowns in black wool crepe and velvet or cashmere overcoats. The color range favors black with contrasting bright yellow, apple green, electric blue, and fuchsia, the whole topped by a tiny pillbox on a frizzy hairstyle. So Sonia.

Nathalie, her daughter, who grew up under the influence, has nevertheless developed a personality of her own. As head designer since 1995, she reworks, varies, and reinterprets the code. The result is colors that are less bright, lines less close to the body, inventive allusions (1930s beach resort), and sensual asymmetries. The fabrics remain fluid, the overlays and transparencies dabble in a more relaxed sexiness. Conscious of the Rykiel legend, Nathalie reissues vintage models, now classic emblems of a highbrow yet liberated femininity.

"Rykiel is more than the Frenchwoman, more than the Parisian. It is the quintessence of the Left Bank spirit."

PAUL SMITH

His style

"Classic with a twist," as he defines it himself. Simple cuts, easy to wear, but in an unexpected color, or with a lining, detail, pocket, or lapel that attract the eye, which intrigue, betray a hint of imagination—especially in menswear. His irregular colored stripes, positioned like a logo, have become a keynote for a million aficionados. He has even "striped" a limited edition of Minis. His sources of inspiration are multiple: music, the world of work, landscape. Moreover, he has written a charming and funny book called *You Can Find Inspiration in Everything (And If You Can't, Look Again)*. Conventional in appearance, his men's suits are actually object lessons in originality: cuts, pleats, lapel inserts, collars, and wristbands. He is not afraid of pink, electric blue, orange, and almond green for men. As befits an Englishman, he likes tweed and checks that he mixes and matches. His women's wear is plainer, in delicate materials, soft monochromes and always featuring a cunning range of patterns—floral, polka dots, or bright stripes resolve into an unexplainable harmony. An airy, casual silhouette, with a touch of irony.

Who is he?

A clothing multimillionaire knighted by Queen Elizabeth in 2000 who had no intention of entering fashion at all. As a teenager his ambition was to become a champion cyclist. His father, a textile merchant had little time for this idea and when he was fifteen had him train in a clothing factory. Unimpressed, Paul's sole pleasure remained the bike trip to work. After two years, he met with a terrible accident on his bike. Six months in hospital and convalescence brought him into contact with circles he found more conducive and he decided to take evening courses in tailoring. His girlfriend, Pauline, who was to become his wife, was a student at fashion school; pooling their savings, they opened a clothing store in Nottingham. The couple had a dog, but masked its stink by squirting Dior's Eau Sauvage around the shop! This was in 1970 and Paul was twenty-four. It was a mere six years later that he presented his debut menswear collection in Paris.

His flair for business and marketing, combined with touches of eccentricity, soon won him customers; not only in England, but also from America to Japan. He had the bright idea of offering more than just clothing in his shops: a whole lifestyle choice, with penknives, notebooks, pens, and many other knick-knacks. It was only in 1998 that this dyed-in-the-wool British male—he has designed for Manchester United—launched his first women's wear collection. The brand today has branched out into a dozen lines, covering every sector, from fragrance to furniture. David Bowie, Tony Blair, and Alain Souchon all have Paul Smith in their closet. In 2007, he returned to his childhood dreams by designing for Rapha, the American cyclewear brand.

"It is not impossible to succeed in business and still try to be a nice person."

GIAMBATTISTA VALLI

His style

Sobriety, uncluttered lines, femininity, and la dolce vita. Such are the words that spring to mind when looking at his collections. One might add: easy-to-wear. His outfits live and breathe comfort and perfectly judged proportions. Few prints and a solid range of colors—be they traditional (black, beige) or bright (emerald, fuchsia). The waist is belted, the bust, small; as flattering as a skirt suit in a Hitchcock film. Valli was born in Rome and lives in Paris, his creations a cross between the Parisienne and the Antonioni heroine. His use of flounces and other ornaments like pleats and gathers is parsimonious. Never too much. He takes his line from the 1950s and 1960s. Inspired by the designers of those years—Carlo Mollino, the Scarpas, Franco Albini—he rounds off sharper edges, avoids all stiffness. He likes black, using it plain or in graphic contrasts. His materials and cuts emphasize the figure. All is neat, spruce, subtly sexy, eternally chic. Like the Cocteau drawings of which he is so fond.

Who is he?

He was born in Rome and was aware of his vocation at an early age, around six or seven. Pulling at the skirts of Caterina, his dressmaking grandmother, he would get her to sew dolls' dresses he'd designed himself. He started in fashion proper at a Rome art school, before taking courses in illustration at Central Saint Martins in London. His first job was with Roberto Capucci, but it was to be with Fendi—where he stayed for six years—that he really learned the ropes. He took up where he left off in 1993, when he was twenty-seven, at the house of Krizia, which entrusted him with its prêt-à-porter lines. Three years later, he joined Emanuel Ungaro in Paris, first as assistant then as creative director for ready-to-wear. In 2004, he launched his own label, which was an immediate hit with clothes-conscious celebs: Sarah Jessica Parker and Victoria Beckham are both fans. Later even the impeccable Queen Rania of Jordan was seen wearing dresses and coats designed by him. Meanwhile, in 2008, the Moncler brand turned to him to modernize its style. Mission successful: in two seasons his glamorous down vests and bomber jackets were all the rage in clubs.

"Timeless, ageless, and effortless: these are the words that for me define style."

VIKTOR & ROLF

Who are they?

The Gilbert and George of fashion! Dutchmen both born in 1969, Viktor Horsting and Rolf Snoeren met at the Academy of Fine Art in Arnhem age twenty, unveiling their joint collection four years later (in 1993) at the now celebrated Festival International de Mode et de Photographie in Hyères, a hotbed of future talent in the South of France. They walked off with first prize. In the wake of this success, they set up a company and hit the headlines in 1998 with an astounding haute couture collection firmly rooted in the aesthetic of the "piece." The media repercussions gave them transcontinental publicity. Their first women's ready-to-wear show followed in 2000, and prêt-à-porter menswear in 2003. Their business heads firmly screwed on, they had meanwhile signed a contract with L'Oréal, allowing them to launch a fragrance, Flowerbomb in 2005 (prohibited at Oslo duty free because the bottle looks like a hand-grenade). After ten years, they earned an exhibition at Paris's Musée de la Mode et du Textile. It should be said that every season's runway show, closer to an art happening than to a presentation of clothing, leaves the public gawping. Their shop in Milan—designed by the Siebe Terrero and Sherrie Zwal tandem—represents an upside-down apartment with the armchairs stuck on the ceiling. But their surrealist imagination conceals a full-blown marketing strategy. Fifteen years after the firm's birth, the duo benefits from a (majority) shareholder of some weight: Renzo Rosso, founder of Diesel, and an avant-garde textile group. And as if to show that one can be at the cutting edge on the runway yet accessible to the man and woman in the street, in 2006 they designed some sixty pieces for H&M. In the same vein, in 2009, they launched a small collection of black dresses, a great classic of fashion heritage, as well as designing luggage for Samsonite. Another exhibit was held in London in 2008, *The House of Viktor & Rolf*, at the Barbican Gallery: fifty-four models presented on dolls.

Their style

In the beginning, they presented a singularly misleading look: two 1960s civil servants, in suit and tie, natty moustaches and horn-rimmed spectacles. Playing fast and loose with convention, they impose the contrasts they choose—as in the 2005 show at which the models started out frighteningly helmeted in black only to metamorphose into romantic fairies on a carpet of roses. Their keynote is opposition: asymmetrical dresses with a giant ruching on the side cut in facets, geometrical tulle underskirts with holes like Swiss cheese or split like Chines lanterns. They take hold of a classic and push it to the limits. For instance, their legendary jacket with multiple lapels like a millefeuille. They inscribe their credo for the season in textile sculptures: "No," "Dream," or in Harlequin diamonds. But beyond all the grandstanding, their clothes reveal perfect control of proportion, an innate sense of balance. There is, perhaps, one constant: flounces arranged flat or in gores, oversized or scattered on a coat, along the neckline, at the bottom of a dress undercut the "well-dressed" look. Friend and fan Tilda Swinton has modeled for them with a leitmotif that sums them up well: "Follow your own path."

"Reality, against which we have only one weapon: the dream."

YOHJI YAMAMOTO

Who is he?

Born in Tokyo, his mother, a dressmaker who brought him up on her own, dreamed he would become a lawyer, so he studied law. In 1966, aged twenty-three, he changed tack, enrolling at the Bunka Fashion College. He started making dresses for his mother's friends and customers, and worked freelance. Thanks to two scholarships, he went to Paris in 1970. Two years later, he founded his label, Y's, for women. Pursuing his experimental clothing, in 1981 he created a more recherché line, Yohji Yamamoto.

The year 1984 saw the arrival of his debut menswear collection. He completed his market portfolio in 2002 with a first ready-to-wear collection. Add a sports collection with Adidas, another with luggage brand Coming Soon, and co-branding with legends such as Doc Martens and Repetto. Curious, highly cultured, and a fan of Bob Dylan, he plays the harmonica as well as guitar in his rock group, and has recorded albums that sell well in Japan, where he is idolized. He has friends in the cinema, designing costumes for several movies by his buddy Takeshi Kitano, including the splendid *Dolls*, and sponsors a karate championship. His daughter, Limi Feu, has followed in her father's footsteps with a label shown in Paris since 2007.

His style

Those in the know call him simply Yohji, because there's no one else doing anything like him. With colleague and ex-girlfriend Rei Kawakubo, founder of Comme des Garçons, he has revolutionized our idea of luxury and elegance through intensive experimentation with fabric, by his taste for black, for asymmetry, and by his constant questioning of the modern Western and Asian idea of feminity. The result: airy garments that are the opposite of "sexy." Moreover, he declares that there is no difference for him between cutting for men and cutting for women: "We are all the same in our souls." He detests the neat, the finished, the trim, and the symmetric, which he considers "tedious and insufficiently human." His first pieces in the 1980s were like costly rags, black, with carefully positioned holes and frayings. Little by little, he has returned to more fitted, more formal structures, with some enthralling forays into color, deep or in luminous dapples. He is not afraid of playing with prints. His cuts have today become classics, with impeccable rectangles or ample, graphic volumes, much more feminine, but without the least concession to prettiness. He continues to engage with black, which he says is "modest and arrogant at the same time. Black is lazy and easy, but mysterious. But above all black says this: I don't bother you—don't bother me."

"In China, they have so many angry young people. To be a fashion designer or an artist, you have to be angry."

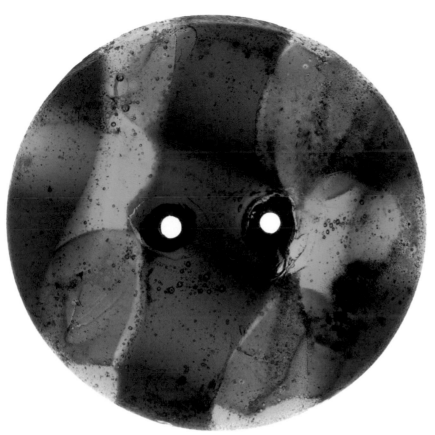

APPENDIXES

ESSENTIAL ACCESSORIES

Even if, by definition, an "accessory" is a supplement to something more important, it can never be regarded as merely secondary. Because in fashion, there are no passengers. How can handbags, scarves, ties, shoes, belts, jewelry, gloves, sunglasses, and hats be considered superfluous? Such details are never "innocent." They reveal your personality or your razor-sharp taste; or else betray a weakness, a slavish obedience to the commands of fashion; or perhaps an idiosyncrasy—in short they are all part of self-display and end up—whether you like it or not—pigeonholing you socially. It's nothing new.

Throughout history, social status has been defined by crowns, diadems, buckles, scepters, and tiaras. Royal and religious dignitaries have marked their dominance with insignia produced by craftsmen "by appointment." The accreditation bestowed on these specialists was the forerunner of today's "label." For example, when the tie appeared in Europe in the seventeenth century, the Sun King marked this new arrival in the male wardrobe by creating the post of royal *cravatier* under the orders of the Master of the Wardrobe. The cravatier thus belonged to the services of the King's Chamber, earning the rank of equerry. The tie promptly ousted the jabot, which itself had supplanted the rigid and uncomfortable ruff. In its wake, European courts were to follow a trend to simplification that went hand in hand with diversity. In the same era, the great Dutch portraitist Van Dyck influenced the aristocracy of his native land, and then the English court, where he set up shop in the 1630s: abandoning Flemish rigor, he exalted shimmering ornaments and accessories, inducing more romantic and unbuttoned attitudes among the English nobility, as well as a penchant for jewelry and ribbons.

Among women, the wind of social change can be gauged by hats. After the Middle Ages and its headwear laden with religious severity—pearly nets, hennins, and horned headdresses hiding the locks—seventeenth- and eighteenth-century fashion indulged in a frenzy of ornamented wigs, in vogue as much among the gents as among the ladies.

Then, finally, the sensual potential of hair—the owner's or "borrowed"—was realized, indeed embraced: ribbons and garlands of flowers, the whole topped by incredible headdresses. Many men shaved their heads, and donned curly powdered wigs crowned with three-cornered hats trimmed with feathers. This was the reign of Rose Bertin, dubbed the "Minister for Fashion" by Marie-Antoinette, and much in demand throughout the courts of Europe. In her Parisian workshops, she devised the most insane hairstyles, bestowing on them humorous names: "lovely hen coiffure," "pouf with feelings," or "fire at the opera house."

WASP AHOY!
The 1970s, Space Age,
and op art fever
by Pierre Cardin.

The eighteenth century was the golden age of accessories, when beavers sleeves; fans (never to be opened in the presence of the queen) with ivory, tortoiseshell, or mother-of-pearl frames; and gloves and veils bespoke of a sophisticated world unconcerned with practicalities, where the preparation of accessories could take hours.

But what matter? Shoes and boots, almost as supple as gloves, often made of silk or velvet, were adorned with bows, precious stones, and embroidery, while men displayed metal buckles on the instep. The French Revolution—and the Terror—put the dampers on all this frivolity. One telltale sign: the top hat was introduced, bringing with it a note of seriousness. Eccentricity went hand in hand with ingenuity: to make it easier to carry the hatter Gibus invented the opera hat, a topper mounted on springs that could be clacked shut and carried under the arm.

Fast forward to the nineteenth century: the daily life of a bourgeois lady was not to be taken lightly and neither they nor their gentlemen would be seen dead without a hat in town. As for the lower orders, the women had to be content with a bonnet and the men with headgear adapted to their trade: beret, cap, or turban.

And what about the handbag? That, too, is no new contraption. In the Middle Ages and during the Renaissance, clothing did not have pockets. To transport money, provisions, a knife, a gift (for the nobility), or even the relics of a saint, a purse of varying size and use, knitted or woven in canvas or imported calico (a printed cotton fabric), and decorated and embroidered to a greater or lesser extent, would be hung with drawstrings from the belt. While today's designers compose accessories in their own right, in the eighteenth century the bag did not yet form part of the ensemble. It was only when dresses became fitted to the body, at the turn of the century, that the highly ornamented reticule became an accessory to be carried with ostentation. In the 1920s, flappers paraded with minaudières, matching makeup bags, ready to powder their nose in public—as fashion demanded.

With the invention of the locomotive in 1804, accessories took on a new lease of life, at once more practical and more visible. Luxury leather goods became a fully fledged trade, while travel meant that less elaborate clothes and accessories were in demand. The advent of true haute couture and then ready-to-wear inaugurated a new era in feminine stylishness. The "collection" gave work to every branch of industry and trade, and an elegant woman's dressing room would have to contain jewelry, shoes, handbags, gloves, hats, and even fragrance and eyeglasses.

FACING PAGE
BAROQUE
A mixture well worth its weight. This Dries Van Noten necklace made up of bracelets of all kinds casts a sideways glance at our love of massive noisy jewelry.

FAN ME DOWN!
Interesting revival of a charming accessory. The fan makes gestures more graceful and attracts the eye to a slender wrist, a shoulder, or a profile. Here, Vuitton fans designed by the actress Rossy de Palma.

FOR MADAM
Metal necklace,
Pierre Cardin.

FOR HISTORY
Silk necktie,
Pierre Cardin.

FOR SIR
Metal tie,
Pierre Cardin.

FOR THE HERITAGE
Genuine silk bowtie,
Brooks Brothers.

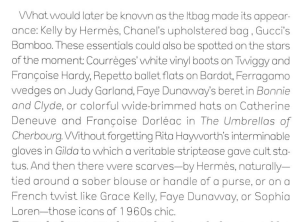

What would later be known as the Itbag made its appearance: Kelly by Hermès, Chanel's upholstered bag , Gucci's Bamboo. These essentials could also be spotted on the stars of the moment: Courrèges' white vinyl boots on Twiggy and Françoise Hardy, Repetto ballet flats on Bardot, Ferragamo wedges on Judy Garland, Faye Dunaway's beret in *Bonnie and Clyde*, or colorful wide-brimmed hats on Catherine Deneuve and Françoise Dorléac in *The Umbrellas of Cherbourg*. Without forgetting Rita Hayworth's interminable gloves in *Gilda* to which a veritable striptease gave cult status. And then there were scarves—by Hermès, naturally—tied around a sober blouse or handle of a purse, or on a French twist like Grace Kelly, Faye Dunaway, or Sophia Loren—those icons of 1960s chic.

From being complements to a style, over the decades, accessories have been promoted into veritable objects of desire that can make or break an entire look.

At the turn of the millennium, the austere lady's suit or classic two-piece for men was offset by a brightly colored pair of shoes or an arty scarf. In the same way, the eternal little black dress was given a twist with an expansive Hervé Van der Straeten or Philippe Ferrandis necklace, an Alaïa leather waist-cinch, or a vintage jeweled belt. Or one might prefer a hint of the exotic with an obi from a Japanese kimono.

As for the bag, its meteoric rise to stardom parallels a sociological development. Not only do bags obsess fashion writers, who have to know exactly *which* It bag is being carried by *which* celeb, but, like the T-shirt, it can trumpet a political stance: "green" (in recycled material), socially committed (spattered with slogans), retro (Chanel, Hermès, Courrèges, Fendi, and Gucci are forever reissuing their backlist), insolently luxurious (in crocodile, python, braided leather, bedecked in rhinestones, tassels and flounces, or handstitched), but especially laden with affectation—be it giant or microscopic. Fully realizing its fabulous commercial potential, fashion houses began to bring out collection after collection of a piece that was once a complementary outlay and now could swallow up the budget of a small country.

Responding to their advertisers, women's magazines contain as many, if not more, pages about accessories as about ready-to-wear. The problem for the consumer is the infernal season-after-season acceleration of products driven out of fashion. In spite of an explosion in price, their fetish value has been devalued. How can one mollycoddle one's bag, gloves, or pumps when the arbiters of fashion

will adjudge them "out" in less than six months? Solutions:

– "No-bag": use pockets or a little ethnic pouch picked up at some exotic destination.

– Vintage: always in style and will acquire value over the years.

– Classic: choose a good article, free of extravagance, with balanced proportions, adapted to your personality and body shape (nothing enormous if you stand five foot high in your stockinged feet), and able to slumber two or three seasons in your closet and still give you delight. You can fall back on a major label with genuine heritage (Chanel, Gucci, Prada, or Hermès), but in general, steer clear of gigantic logos.

– No logo: avoid Vuitton's bag imitating a plastic garbage bag and Chanel's floral crochet 2.55, irremediably dated.

Fendi's famous Baguette bag. Born in 1997, this classic of the Italian house was issued in hundreds of versions. This one is Jungle Fever in velvet and silk brocade, handmade using craft techniques dating from the Renaissance and kept alive by the Lisio Foundation.

Marc Jacobs

MEN, TOO
ABOVE
Prada.
RIGHT
Paul Smith.

An astonishing Vuitton bag decorated by the artist Murakami.

In conclusion, while accessories say more about you than you think, the language has changed. Once upon a time, a woman felt naked without jewelry and gloves; if she carefully matched her shoes and attire, she could still make do with a clutch or a tiny jewel purse. Today, in the context of "fashion simplicity," it is no longer surprising to see an evening gown presented without necklace or earrings; but in reality, no active woman can hope to leave in the morning without an ever-swelling tote bag containing five pounds of datebooks, cell phones, newspapers, cosmetics, jewelry, and maybe even a pair of pumps for the evening. And men are no better off; they haven't the time to change either. They throw on a smart suit in the morning and around 8 p.m. put on a tie—and swap sneakers for oxfords—and hurry off for an elegant dinner. So accessories have gained new importance: essential tools of fashion and comfort, they can save your bacon!

SKIN TO SKIN
A pump by Lanvin with
S&M connotations
whose ankle strap
calls for long, long legs.
Such attention-grabbing
accessories mean one
has to be very careful
with the rest of one's
outfit.

EATEN ALIVE
At once airy, humorous, and perfectly balanced, the well-fitting straw cap of this spider-hat with rhinestone eyes by Marie Mercié means it stays on the head. Marie Mercié is France's most productive and witty designer. Her pieces are collectors' items.

LITTLE LESSONS in fashion

How to recognise...
Pleats

Basic, flat pleats (often iron-formed, usually with crisp edges) for women's attire include the single-fold *knife* pleat, as on the archetypal schoolgirl's grey skirt, while *box* pleats are formed by two knife pleats back to back, providing volume; in *inverted* pleats, the pleat folds inward, toward the body.

The names for elaborate forms that vibrate with light and color can be more poetic: often employed for silk chiffon, *sunray* pleats in bias-cut spread out like rays; an *accordion* pleat is a series of running V-shapes; *broomstick* pleats are not pressed, but loose and wrinkly and formed by twisting the fabric round a pole.

For the more complicated pressed pleats, traditionally the pattern is first drawn out on paper before being reproduced in relief on a double-sided cardboard mold into which the fabric is packed. Forced into a frame, the material is treated with saturated steam in a large oven for approximately an hour at a temperature between 160 and 210°F (70-100°C), depending on the fabric. It is left to cool before being removed from the frame and carefully unfolded. This preeminently French practice supplies plissé pleating for haute couture (ten firms dealing in this craft survive), but for larger volumes and for interior decoration industrial rotary machines are employed.

Natcha Rambova in a Delphos gown by Fortuny, 1924.

Fortuny

The Spanish painter Mariano Fortuny had an abiding passion for clothing. Settling in Venice, together with his wife Henriette, he devised a way of putting fine, irregular, and permanent pleats into silk. In 1908, he used the process for his signature Delphos tea gown: with tiny pleats and holding its shape, it is the tube that slips over the body, the stitching being held in place and weighted by a delicate array of glass beads. The invention even merited a patent. Dyed several times, the iridescently shimmering silk would be retouched by the painter with a brush. Beyond fashion, this revolutionary sobriety remained a success for a period of some forty years. The same smocking process was adopted by others and revisited—in particular by Issey Miyake who also took out patents on his pleats.

Bias and drape

Fabric is composed of a warp and a weft woven together to make poplin, piqué, or crepe. It is this weave that gives "direction" to a material. Bias—sometimes draped—approaches this direction diagonally, to exploit the material's elasticity and avoid cutting (and sewing) the pieces of cloth. Long before our time, the Greeks of antiquity had already explored its potential in creating the toga, an eternal source of inspiration and a constant spur to experimentation. But it was Madeleine Vionnet who, from 1912 to the close of her couture house in 1939, elevated this ancient inspiration into an art form. She would spend hours draping fabric over two-foot high manikins, designing dresses without seams, "because," as she said, "the body doesn't have seams." Her work-

Issey Miyake

A dress in the famous Valentino red.

shops would then make up the life-size gowns. Working on three-dimensional volumes (and not on the flat, as in traditional tailoring) she arranged the three simple forms of square, rectangle, and circle around the female body. Cutting from huge rolls of fabric, with no seams or fastenings, her devastatingly understated dresses shrouded the form in mystery. A woman could simply put it over her head and that was that. Today, the technique remains identical, though with lycra one can work in bias and drape with a fraction of the cloth; a less opulent option. In 1934, Madame Grès, taking her cue from Vionnet, reinforced the fall with silk jersey, a material both heavier and more flexible than silk or satin.

Natural or synthetic fabric?

It is today increasingly difficult to identify fabrics. Tightly twisted yarns, coatings and finishes, or mixed synthetics can produce pliable and soft materials, or rigid and crisp ones. For example, velvet, taffeta, ottoman, and satin can all now be manufactured from either silk, polyester, or cotton. Certain textures can be deceptive: one has to double-check the label to make sure. Polyester knits can feel like cashmere through the fingers, while viscose can imitate silk to perfection.

Why synthetic materials? Primarily because they are low-cost, and the fibers are easier to blend and maintain. For similar reasons, fibers from various sources can be used in conjunction.

According to its origin, a fiber is known as natural, artificial, or synthetic.

An Indian silk (Antik Batik).

Natural animal fibers include:

Wool (sheep), cashmere (goat), alpaca (llama), mohair (angora goat), vicuna, camel, silk (silk worm).

Natural plant fibers include:

Cotton, linen (flax), ramie, sisal, hessian, bamboo, hemp, jute, latex, raffia, coir (coconut).

Artificial fibers:

Obtained by the chemical treatment of natural substances: casein to obtain Lanital, a moth-proof silky-woolly material that doesn't felt; wood cellulose, from pine, bamboo, soya, or birch bark, to obtain glossy, silky, dense viscose, or Modal, the lightest.

Synthetic fibers:

Chemical derivatives of polymers obtained from hydrocarbons or starches. The first plastic fiber was nylon, formulated in 1938. Then came acrylic, polyester, polyamide, polyurethane, and lycra.

GLOSSARY OF KEY FASHION TERMS

B

Ballet flats

Light, colorful, low-front flat shoes (ballerinas), without laces or heels—or with very low heels—that hug the foot, fastened by little cords around the edges. Brigitte Bardot wore her legendary Repettos with everything from capri pants and sheath dresses to a billowing, bias-cut skirt.

Basque

An erotically charged adjunct to the female lingerie box, the basque (or *guêpière*) enabled women to acquire the "wasp-waist" required to squeeze into the tight-waisted jackets of the New Look. It is still alive and kicking today and can be worn instead of a T-shirt beneath a jacket.

Blazer

A navy-blue double-breasted jacket with gilt buttons derived from the uniform of the Royal Navy. The name might come from the name of a British frigate Queen Victoria visited in 1837. In honor of the royal inspection, the captain had blue jackets made for the crew, and, as the sovereign showed her appreciation, the garment was quickly taken up on other vessels.

It is then hardly surprising that it has become a menswear stalwart. The supplier of the Royal Navy—hence of the original blazer—is Gieves 8 Hawkes at 1 Savile Row, London. Snobs may sneer at the gilt buttons—six down the front and four on each wrist!—but those with Royal Navy insignia have a sizable and competitive market of their own.

Bolero

Ravel's celebrated *Boléro* of 1928 is well-known, as are the Mexican bolero "Besame Mucho" (1941), or the searing Cuban version, "Tristeza" (1883), but at the beginning it was a seventeenth-century Spanish dance in three-four time. The bolero jacket originated from the waistcoat without buttons worn by dancers. By the 1930s, these small, ultra-short jackets cropped above the waist started to be worn over evening gowns with plunging necklines. In fur, satin, velvet, or lace, they keep one warm in a light dress without breaking its line or obscuring the waist. Exquisite, of convenient size, the bolero, almost unchanged, remains a timeless and preeminently feminine garment.

Boro

Describes the use of fabrics ("Boro textiles") by (especially) Japanese designers in the 1980s. An "unfinished," ragged look, it was both an acknowledgment of craftsmanship and a homage to materials. This somewhat arty stance ("Boro style") was enthusiastically taken up soon after by a number of Belgian creators.

Borsalino

After training as a hatter in France and Italy, Giuseppe Borsalino opened a store in Alessandria south of Turin in 1957, making a fortune with felt hats manufactured out of hare or rabbit hair. Popularized by the eponymous film, Frank Sinatra, Humphrey Bogart, Robert Redford, Johnny Depp, Michael Jackson (for "Billie Jean"), and Al Capone all found a place for this hat in the locker as it's easy to wear (with broad brim, high crown, middle fold). Italian chic, half-braggadocio, half-distinction, carefully distilled over centuries.

Bourrette silk

Presents irregularities because the yarn is composed of short filaments of silk waste. Its irregular and grainy surface tends to make it a more interesting fabric that than diaphanous silk chiffon.

Brogues

A laced shoe with perforated sewn applications. (The term in French is *richelieu*, for the eponymous cardinal; the word also covers a women's brogue bootee with a rather high heel). *Full brogues* ("*wingtips*") display a serrated, floral pattern all over the toe (in the United States *spectator shoes* are a two-tone variety, often color plus white). A *quarter-brogue* simply has an ornamental dotted line where the front divides from the toe cap. The sober oxford (classic for dress shoes) is an undecorated lace-up shoe that closes completely over the vamp with eyelets beneath; (open-laced) derbys (and bluchers) have lace-eyelets sewn onto the vamp, so the two panels holding the laces open up more fully when the shoe is removed.

C

Cardigan

A long-sleeved knitted jacket whose name is meant to come from the Earl of Cardigan in Wales who, finding his sweater too tight, slashed it down the front with his saber. Choosing jersey and cotton fleece for comfort, agnès b. has popularized an updated version with snap fasteners.

Collar

For men's shirt collars: the Italian has wide points, the tips of the classic (English) collar point down and those of a French collar are elongated. Finally, the *American* collar is button-down.

Crepe

A crinkled, puckered weave that falls splendidly. Wool or silk crepe is slightly rough and almost never creases.

Cut-sewn (*Fr. coupé-cousu*)

Said of a knit treated as though it was woven: the separate elements—of the sweater or cardigan—are sewn together, and not made by increasing or decreasing the knitted stitches into the requisite shape.

F

Flannel

A plain wool, often gray in color, mildly napped. Pants, jacket—or suit—in gray flannel were for long time the favored male apparel, neither too formal nor too unbuttoned. Whatever fashion says, gray flannel remains a mainstay of the male wardrobe.

G

Gingham

A white-and-color check, since Brigitte Bardot made it a 1960s classic, gingham has returned periodically into fashion. Its goody-two-shoes image has been severely tested by Alaïa and Vivienne Westwood.

Guipure

Lacework (point lace) applied to a backing fabric (a mesh, for example), unlike lace that is constitutive of the fabric itself. Dolce & Gabbana and Prada have made guipure fashionable again by exploiting its sexy see-through qualities: "merry widow" over a décolleté or "naughty secretary" buttoned to the throat.

H

Herringbone (pattern)

A zigzag pattern woven in a yarn. A winter tweed jacket with contrasting chevrons in a herringbone pattern is a classic.

Houndstooth

A (twill) weave of contrasting, generally black and white, yarns creating a broken pattern resembling stylized dog's teeth. Often revisited, it's a cloth that never goes out of style.

J

Jacquard and brocade

Jacquards are weaves (in former times, woven on looms invented in the nineteenth century by Joseph Jacquard) that can blend matt and finished yarn or threads of various colors to create a pattern built into the fabric. The back is the exact opposite of the front (face). - Incorporating gilded or silvered thread (e.g., lurex wire), it is called brocade.

L

Leather

Leather (tanned hide) is an important material for fashion products; belts, bags, and shoes, particularly. Prestigious full-grain leather retains its original grainy surface (typical of, for example, Vuitton leather goods). When a hide is sliced down the middle into two sheets, the upper is the top-grain leather, while the lower, fleshside, is split-leather (the "drop"). Both may be surface treated. Scraped on the reverse, nubuck (not invariably made of deer hide) possesses a velvety texture. Suede is the shaggy napped underside of (especially sheep) hide. It is softer than leather proper but not as durable and is often used for coats (especially in 1960s and '70s). Patent leather has been given a high-gloss finish. Various artificial ("faux") leathers exist, including "leather cloth" (originally surface-treated calico) and synthetic leather ("pleather"), essentially polyurethane.

Liberty

A print with a dense pattern of very small flowers. Invented by the Englishman Arthur Lasenby Liberty in 1875, it was a mainstay of Tudor House decor—in particular with the original Tana Lawn design. It was popularized in the 1960s by Cacharel, becoming a classic. A real Liberty of London print can be recognized by the fact that it appears on both sides of the fabric.

Loafer

A casual low slip-on shoe with stitching on the vamp that features a decorative band over the tongue. Its ancestor the moccasin originates among Native Americans. Tod's (often copied) markets loafers in all colors, with the famous nubbed or studded soles, and tassels, turning them into a fashion item.

M

Muslin

The name applied to an ultra-light fabric of loose weave resembling voile. Liquors used to be filtered using cheesecloth. Today dresses, blouses, and scarves are woven in this manner from wool, silk, cotton, and linen.

N

Neck, neckline

Apart from the obvious square, round, and V-necks; there are *draped* necks (with a series of concentric bunches from the neckline and the waterfall (where the material cascades almost down to the stomach). A *crew neck* is round and collarless, typical of the usual T-shirt. A turtleneck is a *high neck* with often a single turn-down, while a roll-neck is similarly close-fitting but may be folded over several times.

P

Pashmina

Pashm means "wool" in Persian. Taken from the name of the semi-wild goat living on the high Tibetan plateau (at a height of more than 4,000 meters), pashmina is a precious wool from its coat spun into ultra-fine yarn to make shawls. The fiber measures less than 15 micrometers thick (a human hair is around 75). A goat produces between 100 and 300 grams of down per year. A true luxury fiber. Imitations are legion, among them, *pattu*, a wool–cotton mix.

Peter Pan collar

A round collar resembling trust of a classic schoolgirl's blouse. A variant with a (sailor's) square section at the back is called a *middy*.

Poplin

The word comes from the French "*papeline*" because the fabric was invented in the papal city of Avignon. In cotton, the fabric presents a fine and tight rib, obtained by the warp thread being finer than the worsted weft. It is the cotton used for luxurious looking shirts.

Prince of Wales check

A variation of check (Glen plaid). The impressionistic pattern results from offsetting a repeat check.

R

Raglan sleeve

One of the two ways of assembling a sleeve. In the raglan, the sleeve and shoulder form a single piece (as in a dolman), the sleeve being sewn on the bias, running from the armhole to the neck, and so providing breadth. Separately sewn on, the seams of regular (or shirt) sleeves follow human morphology, the arm being treated apart. Such an arrangement tends to make the bust appear narrower.

S

Safari jacket

A type of belted khaki jacket with many pouch pockets worn by African colonials. Laced up the front, it was given a sensual twist by Yves Saint Laurent in 1968: a classic.

Style bureaus, trend agencies

These are offices primarily composed of stylists who attempt to forecast trends up to two years in advance. Basing their findings on observations of style and social developments, they shuttle between the world's metropolises on the hunt for the next big thing. For example, the advent of a new femininity, the return of the curvier form, or vogues for ecology or for retro. They then deliver (expensive) "trendbooks"—not only to the clothing industry, but also to

makers of household electrical appliances and even car manufacturers (a domain where their crystal ball needs to see five years ahead). It is an almost exclusively Paris-based profession, the best known being, Promostyl, Nelly Rodi, Mafia, Martine Leherpeur, Trend Union, and Carlin International.

T

T-straps

Also known as *salomes* (after the Jewish princess who performed— in the words of Oscar Wilde— the Dance of the Seven Veils to hoodwink Herod and obtain John the Baptist's head on a platter), these shoes are equipped with a strap attached to the heel that passes through a loop over the foot to form a T-shape in front. Repetto gave a new lease of life to the T-strap with patent leather and heels of various heights.

Taffeta

The word comes from the Persian *taftah*, meaning "woven." In silk—but now also in polyester—the closely woven yarn forms a very fine grain with tiny cross ribs. The material is stiff, iridescent, and crackly, and holds its volume: ideal for evening gowns or chic skirts.

Tie-Dye

A process of hand dyeing— popularized in the West during the 1960s—that consists in twisting the fabric before plunging it into a dye bath.

Tulle

A stiff netting from which underskirts and tutus are made. The name comes from the chief town of the Corrèze, where it was manufactured in the nineteenth century, though the material dates back to the ninth century.

Twill

Woven with parallel diagonal ribs, twill is a splendid stuff that enhances colors, drapes well, and in rayon or silk is lustrous with a pretty fall.

W

Weave

The weave (the way the weft and warp interlock) provides the character of a fabric, its texture. From plain (tabby) weave, the simplest; to more complex variants, among them, satin, twill, taffeta, and jacquard.

Weft and warp

Textile terms designating the yarns making up the *weave* of a fabric: the threads intersect like X and Y coordinates to form a given pattern: herringbone, checks, etc.

WHERE TO SEE FASHION

There are, of course, department stores, which have become veritable temples of contemporary design for so many; then luxury multi-brand outlets impregnated with the owner's taste and personality; and finally designer stores, where the architecture can be as intriguing as the garments on sale. Moreover, any urban center worth its salt today boasts at least one museum of fashion.

MUSEUMS AND INSTITUTIONS

BELGIUM

Mode Museum Provincie Antwerpen (MoMu)
Nationalestraat 28
2000 Antwerp
Tel: + 32 (0)3 470 27 70
www.momu.be

Musée du Costume et de la Dentelle
Rue de la Violette, 12
1000 Brussels
Tel: +32 (0)2 213 44 50
www.bruxelles.be/artdet.cfm/4209
Costume, lace.

CANADA

McCord Museum of Canadian History
690 Sherbrooke Street West
Montreal, Quebec
H3A 1E9
Tel: +1 514 398 7100
www.mccord-museum.qc.ca

Textile Museum of Canada
55 Centre Avenue
Toronto, Ontario
M5G 2H5
Tel: +1 416 599 5321
www.textilemuseum.ca

FRANCE

Cité Internationale de la Dentelle et de la Mode
135 quai du Commerce
62100 Calais
Tel: +33 (0)3 21 00 42 30
www.cite-dentelle.fr
Fashion, lace.

Musée de la Soierie
9 boulevard Leclerc
42190 Charlieu
Tel: +33 (0)4 77 60 28 84
Silk, silk production.

Musée Christian Dior
Rue d'Estouteville
50400 Granville
Tel: +33 (0)2 33 61 48 21
www.musee-dior-granville.com

Musée Textile de Haute-Alsace
Rue du Parc
68470 Husseren-Wesserling
Tel: +33 (0)3 89 38 28 08
www.parc-wesserling.fr/
musee-textile/musee-textile.html

Musée des Tissus et des Arts Décoratifs
34 rue de la Charité
69002 Lyon
Tel: +33 (0)4 72 38 42 00
www.musee-des-tissus.com
Textiles, decorative arts.

Espace Mode Méditerranée
11 la Canebière
13001 Marseille
Tel: +33 (0)4 96 17 06 00
www.espacemodemediterranee.com

Musée de l'Impression sur Étoffes
14 rue Jean-Jacques-Henner
68100 Mulhouse
Tel: +33 (0)3 89 46 83 00
www.musee-impression.com
Fabric prints and printing.

Musée de la Mode et du Textile
107 rue de Rivoli
75001 Paris
Tel: +33 (0)1 44 55 57 50
www.lesartsdecoratifs.fr/francais/
mode-et-textile

Musée Galliera
10 avenue Pierre-Ier-de-Serbie
75016 Paris
Tel: +33 (0)1 56 52 86 00
Fashion since the eighteenth century, documents.

Fondation Pierre-Bergé– Yves-Saint-Laurent
5 avenue Marceau
75016 Paris
Tel: +33 (0)1 44 31 64 00
www.fondation-pb-ysl.net

ITALY
Museo del Tessuto
Via S. Chiara 24
59100 Prato (PO)
Tel: +39 (0)574 611503
www.museodeltessuto.it
Textiles.

UNITED KINGDOM
Victoria & Albert Museum
Cromwell Road
London SW7 2RL
Tel: +44 (0)20 7942 2000
www.vam.ac.uk
The Fashion and Textile Museum
83 Bermondsey Street
London SE1 3XF
Tel: +44 (0)20 7407 8664
www.ftmlondon.org
Fashion Museum
Assembly Rooms
Bennett Street
Bath BA1 2QH
Tel: +44 (0) 1225 477789
www.fashionmuseum.co.uk

Design Museum
Shad Thames
London SE1 2YD
Tel: +44 (0)20 7403 6933
www.designmuseum.org

UNITED STATES
American Textile History Museum
491 Dutton Street
Lowell, Massachusetts 01854
Tel: +1 978 441 0400
www.athm.org
The Metropolitan Museum of Art
1000 Fifth Avenue
New York, New York 10028
Tel: +1 212 535 7710
www.metmuseum.org
The Museum at FIT
Seventh Avenue at 27th Street
New York, New York 10001-5992
Tel: +1 212 217 4558
www.fitnyc.edu/museum

FIDM Museum
919 S. Grand Avenue
Los Angeles, California 90015
Tel: +1 213 624 1201
www.fidmmuseum.org
Los Angeles Country Museum of Art
5905 Wilshire Blvd
Los Angeles, California 90036
Tel: +1 323 857 6000
www.lacma.org
Phoenix Art Museum
1625 N Central Ave
Phoenix, Arizona 85004
Tel: +1 602 257 1880
www.phxart.org
Museum of Fine Arts, Houston
1001 Bissonnet St
Houston, Texas 77005
Tel: +1 713 639 7300
www.mfah.org

FESTIVAL

Festival International de Mode et de Photographie
Villa Noailles
Montée Noailles
83400 Hyères
Tel: +33 (0)4 98 08 01 98
www.villanoailles-hyeres.com
Held for a few days in April and May.

TRADE SHOWS, EVENTS, FAIRS

Fashion shows held by the French Federation
   of Couture and Prêt-à-Porter, Paris
Fashion Week, London
Fashion Week, New York
Prêt-à-porter salons, Paris
Salon Première Classe, Paris (accessories)
Salon Who's Next in Paris (new trends)
Salon Who's Next in Dubai
Milano Moda Donna
Milano Moda Uomo
Saloni Pitti, Milan
Milano Unica (new trends)

WHERE TO LEARN A FASHION TRADE

Fashion design is not all there is to fashion. The sector comprises a host of technical and artistic branches, as well as marketing and management. France is well endowed with specialized schools, some of which, in particular ESMOD, have branches abroad. British and American schools enjoy a solid reputation for the commercial side of the business. Those, too, have branches in France: Parsons, for instance.

BELGIUM

Koninklijke Academie Antwerpen
(fashion department)
Mutsaertstraat 31 2000 Antwerp
Tel: +32 2 506 10 10
info@arba-esa.be
www.arba-esa.be

École Nationale Supérieure des Arts Visuels de la Cambre
21, rue de l'Abbaye de la Cambre
21.1050 Brussels
Tel: +32 2 626 17 80
lacambre@lacambre.be
www.lacambre.be

FRANCE

Studio Berçot
29 rue des Petites Écuries
75010 Paris
Tel: +33 (0)1 42 46 15 55
studiobercot@orange.fr
www.studio-bercot.com

Atelier Chardon Savard
✿ 15 rue Gambey
75011 Paris
Tel: +33 (0)1 43 14 02 22
info@acs-paris.com
www.atelier-chardon-savard.com

✿ 31–33 rue Saint Léonard
44000 Nantes
nantes@acs-paris.com
www.chardon-savard-nantes.com

Lisaa Mode (Institut Supérieur des Arts Appliqués)
55 rue du Cherche-Midi
75006 Paris
Tel: +33 (0)1 42 22 13 01
www.lisaa.com

ESMOD
12 rue de La Rochefoucauld
75009 Paris
Tel: +33 (0)1 44 83 81 50
paris@esmod.com
www.esmod.com

Esaa-Duperré
(École Supérieure des Arts Appliqués)
11 rue Dupetit-Thouars
75003 Paris
Tel: +33 (0)1 42 78 59 09
direction@duperre.org
www.duperre.org

École Nationale Supérieure des Arts Décoratifs
31 rue d'Ulm
75240 Paris cedex 05
Tel: +33 (0)1 42 34 97 00
www.ensad.fr

ECSCP (École de la Chambre Syndicale de la Couture Parisienne)
119 rue Réaumur
75002 Paris
Tel: +33 (0)1 42 61 00 77
Email: ecole@modeaparis.com
www.modeaparis.com/vf/ecoles

IFM (Institut Français de la Mode)
36 quai d'Austerlitz
75013 Paris
Tel: +33 (0)1 70 38 89 89
management@ifm-paris.com
creation@ifm-paris.com
www.ifm-paris.com

Esiv (École Supérieure des Industries du Vêtement)
73 boulevard Saint-Marcel
75013 Paris
Tel: +33 (0)1 40 79 92 60
www.esiv.fr

ITALY

Domus Academy
Via G. Watt 27
21143 Milano
Tel: + 39 (0)2 42 41 40 01
info@domusacademy.it
www.domusacademy.com

JAPAN
Bunka Fashion College
3-22-1, Yoyogi, Shibuya-Ku
Tokyo
Tel: +81 3 32 99 20 57
www.bunka-fc.ac.jp

UNITED KINGDOM
**Central Saint Martins College of Art
and Design**
Southampton Row
London WC1B 4AP
Tel: +44 (0)20 7514 7022
info@csm.arts.ac.uk
www.csm.arts.ac.uk
Royal College of Art (RCA)
Darwin Building, Kensington Gore
London SW7 2EU
Tel: +44 (0)20 7590 4444
info@rca.ac.uk
www.rca.ac.uk
London College of Fashion
20 John Princes Street
London W1G 0BJ
Tel: +44 (0)20 7514 7400
www.fashion.arts.ac.uk

UNITED STATES
Fashion Institute of Technology (FIT) New York
Seventh Avenue at 27th Street
New York, New York 10001–5992
Tel: +1 212 217 7999
www.fitnyc.edu/museum
Parsons School of Design New York
66 Fifth Avenue
New York, New York 10011
Tel: +1 212 229 8900
www.parsons.newschool.edu
Fashion Institute of Design and Merchandising
919 South Grand Avenue
Los Angeles, CA 90015–1421
Tel: +1 800 624 1200
www.fidm.edu

Dresses by Carven (left)
and Rabih Kayrouz (above).

INDEX OF PROPER NAMES

Three classics that are forever being reinterpreted for both sexes: agnès b.'s snap cardigan, Cacharel's Liberty pattern shirt, and army jackets.

SELECTED BIBLIOGRAPHY

BARTHES, ROLAND.
The Fashion System.
Berkeley:
University of California Press,
1990.

COLENO, NADINE.
The Hermes Scarf:
History and Mystique.
London:
Thames 8 Hudson,
2010.

DIOR, CHRISTIAN.
The Little Dictionary
of Fashion: A Guide to Dress
Sense for Every VVoman.
London:
V 8 A Publishing,
2008.

HESSE, JEAN-PASCAL.
Pierre Cardin:
60 Years of Innovation.
Paris:
Assouline,
2010.

LAULHÈRE-VIGNEAU,
CATHERINE, ED.
Parisiennes: A Celebration
of French VVomen.
Paris:
Flammarion,
2007.

MÜLLER, FLORENCE.
Art and Fashion.
London:
Thames 8 Hudson,
2000.

MÜLLER, FLORENCE
AND YVONNE DESLANDRES.
Fashion Game Book:
A VVorld History
of 20th-Century Fashion.
Paris:
Assouline,
2008.

MÜLLER, FLORENCE
AND FARID CHENOUNE.
Yves Saint Laurent.
New York:
Harry N. Abrams,
2010.

RUPPERT, JACQUES.
Le Costume Français.
Paris:
Flammarion,
1996.

GUNDLACH, F.C.
F.C. Gundlach: Photographic VVork.
Göttingen:
Steidl,
2010.

Photographic credits

Antik Batik/Thierry Le Goues: p. 241; Archives du 7e Art/All Rights Reserved: p. 52, 64, 76; Archives Alaïa: p. 37; Archives Pierre Cardin: p. 115, 118 right, 233, 236 right; Flammarion Archives: p. 19, 28, 36, 38, 42, 56, 68, 72, 83, 84, 86, 112, 113, 139, 140, 153, 155, 167, 189, 197, 215, 237 bottom, 240, 249; Archives Alexis Mabille: p. 53; Archives Thierry Mugler: p. 29, 119 left; Archives Prada: p. 109, 130, 217, 237 top left; © Archives Sonia Rykiel: p 147; Archives Giambattista Valli: p. 225; © Michel Arnaud/CORBIS: p. 172, 173; Pierre Bairin: p. 204; © Matteo Bazzi/epa/Corbis: p. 138; Biasion Studio/Wirelmage: p. 176; Exposition Fondation Mona Bismarck, photo Michel Azouz: p. 230 top; Exposition Fondation Mona Bismarck, collection Loïc Allio: p. 230 bottom, 231; Alban Boireau (JUSTE DEBOUT, Worldwide Street Dance Festival, Bercy, 2009): p. 91; Jacques Bosser: p. 93; Chanel/Photo Karl Lagerfeld, p. 209; Thierry Chomel: p. 212; Ossie Clark/Vietnam/1969: p. 163; Condé Nast Archive: p. 116 left; © Condé Nast Archive/Corbis: p. 22; Courtesy of Armani: p. 174; Courtesy of Cacharel: p. 251 center, 255 center; Courtesy of Comme des Garçons: p. 183; Courtesy of E2: p. 180, 181; Courtesy of Fendi: p. 237 top; Courtesy of Alberta Ferretti: p. 190; Courtesy of Fishbone: p. 92; © Shoji Fujii: p. 205; Courtesy of Harrods: p. 159; Courtesy of Anne Valérie Hash: p. 134, 198, 199; Courtesy of Marc Jacobs: p. 200, 201, 237 center right; Courtesy of Rabbih Kayrouz: p. 197, 249 right; Courtesy of Sophia Kokosalakis: p. 206, 207; Courtesy of Lanvin: p. 135, 186, 187, 238; Courtesy of Alexander Mc Queen: p. 50, 88-89, 210, 211; Courtesy of Phoebe Philo: p. 214; Courtesy of Rodarte: p. 219; Courtesy of Frank Sorbier: p. 256; Courtesy of Valentino: p. 241 top; Courtesy of Dries Van Noten: p. 141, 213; © Photo B.D.V./CORBIS: p. 107; Frank Christen: p. 202; Photography by Philippe Dalmas © S. Weiss/Rapho/Eyedea Illustration: p. 161; Jean-Philippe Decros: p. 149; © Julio Donoso/Sygma/Corbis: p. 44, 49; All Rights Reserved: p. 32, 33, 35, 39, 57, 105, 117 left, 119 right, 185, 218; All Rights Reserved/Greg Kessler: p. 47 right; Raphaël Elicha: p. 31; Monica Feudi: p. 47 left, 229; Stéphane Grangier: p. 178; F. C. Gundlach: p. 117 right, 118 left; Jacques Habbah: p. 171; Horst: p. 116 right; © kazou ohishi: p. 170; Koichi Inakoshi: p. 228; Karl Lagerfeld: p. 194; Karl Lagerfeld, self-portrait, 2009 : p. 208; Olivier Lecomte/www.olivierlecomte.com: p. 80; Dominique Muitre: p. 179; Guy Marineau: p. 57, 101, 165; © Olivier Marty/Robert Laffont: p. 43; Jamie McCarthy/Wirelmage: p. 196; Antonio de Moraes Barros Filho/Wirelmage: p. 190; Nadji chez Didier Ludot: p. 121; © Orban Thierry/Corbis Sygma: p. 45, 151, 227; Petit Bateau: p. 40; Photo12.com—Scala, Florence: p. 60; Nathalie Prébende: p. 1-12, 54, 55, 58, 59, 62, 63, 66, 67, 70, 71, 74, 75, 78, 79, 94, 95, 96, 97, 120, 122, 123, 124, 125, 126, 127, 128, 129, 156, 168, 235, 251 top, 251 bottom, 255; Rabbani and Solimene Photography/Wirelmage: p. 172; © RMN (musée Guimet, Paris) / All Rights Reserved: p. 25; © RMN/Jean-Gilles Berizzi: p. 24; Anne Roman: p. 239; Eiichiro Sakata: p. 182; © Sonia Rykiel, photo Frédérique Dumoulin: p. 221; © Sonia Rykiel, photo Taro Terazawa: p. 220; Jewel Samad: p. 114; Paul Smith: p. 16, 69, 137 right, 222, 223, 236 left, 237 bottom left; Terry Smith/Time Life Pictures/Getty Images: p. 145; Patrice Stable for Jean Paul Gaultier: p. 23, 27, 77, 137 left, 192, 193; studio agatha ruiz de la prada: p. 32 right, 142; Studio des fleurs: p. 87, 110; © Frank Trapper/Corbis: p. 85; © Pierre Vauthey/CORBIS SYGMA: p. 103; Willy Venderperre: p. 184; Venturelli/Wirelmage: p. 226; Viktor & Rolf/Peter Stigter: p. 21; Courtesy of Vuitton: p. 234, 237 bottom right; Kasia Wandzyc/Paris Match/Scoop: p. 191; Albert Watson: p. 216; © WWD/Condé Nast/Corbis: p. 41, 43, 48, 61, 65, 73, 133 bottom left, 133 top right, 133 top left, 133 bottom right, 175, 177, 195.

Learning Resources Centre
Middlesbrough College
Dock Street
Middlesbrough
TS2 1AD

Acknowledgments

The author would like to thank Élisabeth Couturier for her considerate, considered, and ever positive attitude; François Huertas for his creativity and humor, and generously provisioned wardrobe; Nathalie Prébende for a gentleness combined with stamina; Julie Rouart for her buoyant mood and her dynamism; Camille Giordano for her engaging curiosity and hard work; and for their wardrobes, true storehouses of invention and passion: Cathy Mespoulède, Florence BenSadoun, Marie and Bernard Besançon, Andrew Streeter and Patrice Pujol, Françoise Dupertuis, Anne-Valérie Hash, Didier Ludot, and Firouz for the patience and encouragement of a novelist who knows all about the long haul that is book-writing. And finally all those I have forgotten in my enthusiasm.

François   Catherine   Julie   Camille   Élisabeth   Marie   Nathalie

Translated from the French by David Radzinowicz
Copyediting: Helen Woodhall
Design: François Huertas
Typesetting: Thierry Renard
Proofreading: Chrisoula Petridis
Color Separation: Reproscan
Printed in Italy by Graphart

Originally published in French as *Fashion: Mode d'Emploi*
© Flammarion, S.A., Paris, 2010

English-language edition
© Flammarion, S.A., Paris, 2011

87, quai Panhard et Levassor
75647 Paris Cedex 13

editions.flammarion.com

11 12 13   3 2 1

ISBN: 978-2-08-030169-7

Dépôt légal: 03/2011

FOLLOWING PAGE
THE HAPPY COUPLE
SAINT-PAUL-DE-VENCE
(Summer 2008)
Lace-clad maiden
in miniskirt with her
childhood sweetheart
in a tuxedo jacket with
matching bermudas
and black socks. Franck
Sorb designs for tours
by Madonna and
Mylène Farmer, as well
as for the Paris Opera.
All his pieces are unique.